ECONOMIES WITH MANY AGENTS

Economies with Many Agents

An Approach Using Nonstandard Analysis

SALIM RASHID

The Johns Hopkins University Press Baltimore and London

Printed in the United States of America

The Johns Hopkins University Press
701 West 40th Street
Baltimore, Maryland 21211
The Johns Hopkins Press Ltd., London

The paper used in this publication meets the minimum requirements of American National Standard for Information Sciences—Permanence of Paper for Printed Library Materials, ANSI Z39.48-1984.

LIBRARY OF CONGRESS CATALOGING-IN-PUBLICATION DATA

Rashid, Salim, 1949-   .
Economies with many agents.

Bibliography: p.
Includes index.
1. Microeconomics—Mathematical models. 2. Economics, Mathematical. I. Title.
HB1725.R37 1987 330'.01'51 86-45442
ISBN 0-8018-3379-5 (alk. paper)

To My Parents

Contents

Figures

Preface

This book aims primarily at introducing nonstandard analysis to economists; I hope it will also attract mathematicians interested in mathematical economics. I firmly believe that nonstandard analysis is a (relatively) new mathematical tool that is at once intuitive, simple, and powerful. All mathematical methods that economists apply are, after all, meant to be no more than means by which to render economic intuitions precise. If the mathematics is so weak that it cannot prove our intuitive beliefs, it should, of course, be rejected as inadequate for the purpose at hand. If, however, the mathematics employed is so powerful as to give rise to problems that have no clear economic content, then we should, perhaps, reassess our options. A failure to realize the latter issue has, in my opinion, clouded some facets of mathematical economics. It is my belief that nonstandard analysis is entirely adequate for the questions economists ask, giving rise to a minimum of mathematical problems with negligible economic content, that has led me to write this small book.

The economic topic chosen to illustrate my thesis is by now a familiar one—economies with many agents. As such, it should be accessible not only to research workers and graduate students but also to advanced undergraduates who are familiar with such books as Werner Hildenbrand and Alan P. Kirman's *Introduction to Equilibrium Analysis* (1976). The principal problems to be discussed were raised by economists, and the earliest attempts to make these intuitions rigorous are discussed in chapter 1, which is meant to motivate the reader. These economic problems have been named after their originators and are called Farrell's conjectures and Edgeworth's conjectures. They are dealt with at length after the reader has been introduced to nonstandard analysis and nonstandard economies in chapters 2, 3, 4, and 5. The two final chapters are meant to relate nonstandard methods to other approaches used in the literature. In one of them it is shown that nonstandard proofs sometimes possess a magical property—they disappear and return as entirely standard proofs. One such example is treated carefully in this chapter. The final chapter is perhaps the only polemical chapter of this volume. I begin by showing that, for a certain class of economies, the economic behavior of measure-theoretic and nonstandard economies is equivalent; thereafter, the advantage of nonstandard analysis in proving asymptotic results and in modeling situations in which individuals are significant is pointed out. Some notes on a variety of other results on nonstandard economies precede the bibliography.

I am grateful to Carol Halliday and the WPC for an excellent job of typing and to Anders Richter, Trudie Calvert, and Nancy West for helping me through the difficult process of making a manuscript publishable. I also wish to thank the Econometric Society and Academic Press for permission to quote from *Econometrica* and the *Journal of Economic Theory*, respectively.

This book was originally conceived and planned as a joint effort with M. Ali Khan. Over the years he has been both friend and mentor, and I greatly regret that he is no longer actively working in this field, since it has necessitated my becoming the sole author of this book. He has given me his wholehearted assistance throughout the writing of this volume, and I am deeply grateful for his encouragement and help. If Donald J. Brown had not extended a sympathetic hand I know I would never have done any research in nonstandard analysis. Only graduate students know the emptiness of the thesis hunt, and I am forever indebted to Don Brown for the kind way he guided me during the writing of my dissertation.

My wife, Zeenet, and my sons, Shahid, Sabir, and Imran, have patiently borne with me during my attempt at authorship. My debt to them, of course, extends far beyond anything written here.

Reader's Guide

To make this volume as accessible as possible, I would like to emphasize that the basic definitions of the model, plus the equilibrium notions, are repeated anew in each chapter. Readers with some knowledge of the literature should thus feel free to start reading wherever their interest leads them. Those who are approaching the subject for the first time should read all of chapters 1 through 5, with varying degrees of concentration, depending upon their backgrounds in economics and mathematics. Thereafter, the following is an indication of the level of difficulty of the remaining chapters, with chapters 6 and 8 being the easiest and chapter 12 the hardest: chapters 6 and 8, chapter 9, chapter 11, chapters 7 and 10, chapter 12. The reader, one hopes, will then be both willing and prepared to examine the most recent uses of nonstandard models in economics, some guide to which is provided in the Bibliographic Note. Results are listed serially within each chapter. Results proved earlier are referred to by chapter, then result; for example, in chapter 7, Theorem 2 refers to the second theorem of that chapter and Theorem 5.5 refers to the fifth theorem of chapter 5.

I

NONSTANDARD ANALYSIS AND LARGE ECONOMIES

1 Why Large Economies?

This chapter attempts to motivate the study of economies with an infinite number of agents by showing that they satisfy our intuitive concept of "perfect competition" and that they possess certain regularities not found in finite economies. We study such economies not because they are considered as existent realities, but rather because infinite economies provide a guide to the behavior of large but finite economies. Questions of considerable interest to economists, such as the pricing out of Pareto-optimal allocations with nonconvex preferences, are seen to possess satisfactory answers in such a framework. Of course, having proved results for infinite economies, we will then have to see what such results imply for the behavior of finite economies.

No specific prerequisites are laid down for this chapter. The reader is advised to read through to the end of the chapter because the exposition proceeds at two levels. In the first half the discussion proceeds at a general, and hence more abstract, level; in the second half the questions raised earlier are illustrated more concretely. Consequently, it is hoped that queries raised by obscurities in the first half are clarified in the second half.

I do not, of course, claim that the applications described here are the only reasons for studying large economies.

The reader is asked to understand that, although the notation used in this chapter is generally consistent with that used in the formal proofs later, there are small differences.

The Main Problems

The principal economic model I consider in this volume is that of Walrasian general equilibrium. The belief that economic phenomena should ultimately derive from the behavior of individuals lies at the heart of the theory of general equilibrium and perhaps explains why the ideas of Leon Walras have achieved such prominence in recent decades. Even though aggregative models are indispensable for policy purposes, models that treat the individual as the ultimate unit of analysis possess an aesthetic appeal lacking in aggregated models that speak of "consumption," "investment," and so on as though they were mechanical properties of an economy. Aesthetic appeal is not, however, the only reason for considering disaggregated models; even those who believe such detailed models to be needless abstractions will concede that results true for them will normally be true for *all* aggregate models, and hence there is considerable economy of effort in proving results once which will then apply to all aggregative models.

It is useful to introduce the principal questions asked by students of general equilibrium by considering the traditional distinction between positive and normative economics. As positive economists we attempt to state what will happen; for example, if a tax is charged, will more be sold? As normative economists we attempt to evaluate various economic positions; for example, will there be a net gain if a monopolistic industry is broken up into many small firms? The primary method by which positive questions, such as the impact of taxes, are assessed is to find out the position of market equilibrium before the tax and to see how it changes after the tax. For such a procedure to be meaningful it is essential that equilibrium exist. To judge whether it is necessary to intervene in the operations of the market, that is, for normative questions, one must know whether the equilibria reached in an unfettered market possess any desirable qualities. The two questions that have perhaps occupied general equilibrium theorists the most have therefore been related to conditions that ensure the existence of a general equilibrium and a study of the normative efficiency of such equilibria. In the simplest economies, in which no production takes place and only exchange is permitted, it can be shown that convexity of preferences is sufficient not only to ensure the existence of an equilibrium price vector but also to enable any Pareto-optimal allocation to be achievable as a market equilibrium, provided lump-sum transfers are permitted.

Beginning with the systematic mathematization of economics in the late nineteenth century, it was recognized that fairly restrictive assumptions were needed to prove intuitively plausible economic results. For example, the only tractable way to model the entire economy seemed to require the assumption that all agents, both consumers and producers, are perfect competitors. Thus every agent was supposed to assume that his own actions would have no impact upon the market. Now, even if the agent in question is one of a thousand identical firms, it seems plausible to argue that the individual would have a finite impact, say one-thousandth of the quantity sold, and so the belief of the agent is false. And an agent will continue to have a nonzero impact in any finite economy, no matter how large. The only way for an agent to have a truly negligible impact is to assume that the economy contains an infinite number of agents. Economies with infinitely many agents thus turn out to be the natural model for the institution of "perfect competition."[1]

Before long, economists realized that such infinite economies possessed further desirable features. In finite economies, economists have assumed convexity of consumer preferences to prove the existence of a competitive equilibrium. As Robert Aumann (1964) remarked, mathematical economists had known that convexity of individual preferences was not strictly necessary; convexity in the aggregate would suffice. For economies with a finite number of consumers, however, there was no natural way of obtaining aggregate convexity other than by imposing convexity on individuals. M. J. Farrell (1959) conjectured that economies having an infinite number of agents would possess a competitive equilibrium even if individual preferences were not convex; furthermore, Farrell argued persuasively that any Pareto-optimal allocation in the infinite economy would be achievable as a market equilibrium. Farrell's conjectures on the dispensability of convexity in infinite economies form the first set of topics motivating the study of infinite economies.

Infinite economies gain further significance in providing a link with game theory. Modern general equilibrium theory is noncooperative because it considers only those equilibrium allocations that arise when consumers ignore the possibility of trading directly with each other; instead, individuals are assumed to accept the prices announced by, and to trade

1. This point was eloquently made by R. J. Aumann (1964) in his pioneering article:

> The notion of perfect competition is fundamental in the treatment of economic equilibrium. The essential idea of this notion is that the economy under consideration has a "very large" number of participants, and that the influence of each individual participant is "negligible." Of course, in real life no competition is perfect; but, in economics, as in the physical sciences, the study of the ideal state has proved very fruitful, though in practice it is, at best, only approximately achieved.
>
> Though writers on economic equilibrium have traditionally assumed perfect competition, they have, paradoxically, adopted a mathematical model that does not fit this assumption. Indeed, the influence of an individual participant on the economy cannot be mathematically negligible, as long as there are only finitely many participants. Thus a mathematical model appropriate to the intuitive notion of perfect competition must contain infinitely many participants. (P. 39)

directly with, the "market." As originally formulated by Leon Walras (1874), the paradigm is the floor of a stock exchange, where an auctioneer announces prices, receives information on individual demands and supplies, and adjusts prices so as to achieve equilibrium. This is a far cry from an equilibrium being determined by the conjunction of a multitude of bargains between consumers, implicit in Adam Smith's phrase "the higgling of the market." F. Y. Edgeworth (1881) suggested an equilibrium notion that did not depend on prices or price-taking behavior—that is, the core of an economy. The core is the set of all outcomes that cannot be improved upon by any subset of traders, who are permitted to trade among themselves. The core is thus a cooperative solution concept that permits direct bargains between agents. In terms of the familiar two-person Edgeworth box, the core is precisely that part of the contract curve that is preferred by both consumers to their initial endowments.

In general, the core will contain the set of competitive equilibria. Edgeworth, however, conjectured that as the size of the economy grew, the core would shrink until it became identical with the set of competitive equilibria. This may be considered as stating that, in a perfectly competitive economy in which each individual has an infinitesimal fraction of the total endowment, every allocation stable under bargaining—in the core—can be sustained as a competitive equilibrium. The conjecture was proved for the case of transferable utilities by Martin Shubik (1959), then significantly generalized to the nontransferable case by Herbert Scarf (1962), and the proof simplified later by Gerard Debreu and Herbert Scarf (1963). Debreu and Scarf's result showed that if an economy with a finite number of agents was replicated, the core of each replication was smaller than the core of the original economy; the set of competitive equilibria, however, remains the same for all replications, and Debreu and Scarf showed that, as the replications grew without bound, the core shrank until it eventually coincided with the set of equilibria. The concept of having an infinitesimal share of an economy's endowment is, however, impossible to formalize in finite economies, and the identity of the set of core allocations and the set of competitive equilibria was established only when economies with a continuum of agents was considered. Edgeworth's conjecture about infinite economies is thus significant because it links together noncooperative price-taking behavior and cooperative bargaining behavior.

A significant step toward making the concept of the core realistic, and thereby heightening the importance of Edgeworth's conjecture, was taken by David Schmeidler (1972), who showed that the core remains unchanged if only coalitions that are smaller than a preassigned size are allowed to form. The preassigned upper bound may be arbitrarily small. This is important because costs will clearly prohibit the viability of coalitions that form a significant portion of the economy. This point takes on added force in very large economies because it is far more unrealistic to expect that all coalitions of size ninety thousand can form in an economy of size one hundred thousand than it is to assume that all coalitions of size ninety can form in an economy with one hundred agents, even though the sizes of both sets of coalitions are proportionately the same in both the economies. Karl Vind (1972) then showed that the core is still unchanged if a lower bound is placed on the size of blocking coalitions. Brigit Grodal (1972) rounded out this line of argument by establishing not only that only small coalitions can safely be considered, but further, that the coalitions need only be formed by using essentially a finite set of types of traders. The results of Schmeidler, Vind, and Grodal were exactly true only for infinite economies. Using nonstandard analysis, Khan (1976) soon derived the implications of these results for large, finite economies. Subsequently, Khan and Rashid (1978) extended the earlier results to cover cores with costs of coalition formation. Provided these costs—for example, the bargaining costs—were monotonic and continuous, because it took more time and resources to form larger coalitions and that it cost only slightly more to form a slightly larger coalition, then all the core allocations that could form under such conditions could also be approximately sustained by a price system. Khan and Rashid's result has the following economic interpretation: Let us make it costly to form coalitions, and let us simultaneously make it costly to operate markets; for example, let there be a lump sum charged from each trader to cover costs of operating the market. Then for large, finite economies any allocation obtained by the cooperative mechanism of the core could equally well have been obtained by using the noncooperative mechanism of the market.

Rigorous proofs of both Farrell's conjectures, on optimality and existence without convexity, and Edgeworth's conjecture, on the coincidence of the core and competitive equilibria, have been provided by several authors in recent years. The mathematical tools chiefly employed thus far belong to a branch of mathematics known as measure theory. An alternative branch of mathematics exists, however, known as nonstandard analysis, which can also be used to study the properties of economies with an infinite number of traders. Nonstandard analysis performs operations on infinite sets entirely analogously to operations on finite sets. In courses on integration, it is said that integration is "like" summation, only over infinite sets. Using nonstandard analysis, integration over infinite sets *is* summation. Expositional ease, however, is not the only reason for studying nonstandard analysis.

Most economists are skeptical of results that are stated only for economies with infinitely many traders. To be interesting, approximate forms of these results must also be true for large but finite economies.[2] This is a fundamental requirement that cannot be overemphasized. To obtain such approximating results, the measure-theoretic school appeals to the theory of weak convergence, whereas nonstandard analysts apply a metamathematical principle which guarantees that results proved to be true for all suitably formulated infinite economies must hold true in approximate form for all large, finite economies, the degree of approximation improving as the economies get larger. Both the ease of formulating the infinite economy and the readiness with which finite analogues of the infinite results can be found suggest a need for careful study of large economies using nonstandard analysis.

Farrell's Conjectures

In 1959 M. J. Farrell proved some fundamental results regarding the role of convexity assumptions in the theory of competitive markets. Subse-

2. The following quote from Aumann (1964) is long but worth careful study because it points out distinctly that infinite economies are justified as technical means of approximating large but finite economies:

> The idea of a continuum of traders may seem outlandish to the reader. Actually, it is no stranger than a continuum of prices or of strategies or a continuum of "particles" in fluid mechanics. In all these cases, the continuum can be considered an approximation to the "true" situation in which there is a large but finite number of particles (or traders or strategies or possible prices). The purpose of adopting the continuous approximation is to make available the powerful and elegant methods of the branch of mathematics called "analysis," in a situation where treatment by finite methods would be much more difficult or even hopeless (think of trying to do fluid mechanics by solving n-body problems for large n).
>
> There is perhaps a certain psychological difference between a fluid with a continuum of particles and a market with a continuum of traders. Though we are intellectually convinced that a fluid contains only finitely many particles, to the naked eye it still looks quite continuous. The economic structure of a shopping center, on the other hand, does not look continuous at all. But, for the economic policy maker in Washington, or for any professional macroeconomist, there is no such difference. He works with figures that are summarized for geographic regions, different industries, and so on; the individual consumer (or merchant) is as anonymous to him as the individual molecule is to the physicist.
>
> Of course, to the extent that individual consumers or merchants are in fact not anonymous (think of General Motors), the continuous model is inappropriate, and our results do not apply to such a situation. But, in that case, perfect competition does not obtain either. (P. 41)

It follows, of course, that unless one is willing to accept on faith that infinite models necessarily provide approximations to large, finite economies, results proved for infinite economies must be followed by further theorems relating the infinite economy to a large but finite economy. A failure to grasp the importance of the asymptotic results embedded within the infinite economy framework led Georgescu-Roegen (1979, 1981) to some misleading criticisms of this literature.

quently, Jerome Rothenberg (1960) clarified and extended several of Farrell's arguments, and the significance of the entire issue was debated by F. M. Bator (1961), Farrell (1959, 1961), T. C. Koopmans (1961), and Rothenberg (1961).[3] The subsequent literature on nonconvexities owes much to these seminal contributions, but it is unfortunate that the importance of these intuitively appealing arguments has been cast into shade by later developments.

Perhaps the most important reason why Farrell's and Rothenberg's arguments have been neglected is that they actually prove something very different from that which they claim to have proved. Farrell, for example, explicitly states at the beginning of his article that he wishes to see whether competitive equilibria remain Pareto-optimal in the presence of nonconvexities: "The object of this paper is to examine how far the allocation of resources brought about by a perfectly competitive market remains optimal when indifference maps and production functions cease to be convex" (1959:377). In this interpretation, Farrell is entirely followed by Rothenberg. It was only when Koopmans pointed out that the problem being explicitly tackled was trivial—because if a competitive equilibrium exists, it is Pareto-optimal without any need for convexity assumptions—that Farrell seems to have realized that he had actually provided persuasive arguments for the existence of a competitive equilibrium in markets in which "the numbers of both producers and consumers are indefinitely large." He does not, however, go beyond asserting that his arguments are relevant to the problem of the existence of a competitive equilibrium. Farrell correctly sensed that the crucial point, for both the problems of optimality and existence, is to establish the approximate convexity of the average of a sum of sets.

The situation that aroused Farrell was a diagram used by J. V. de Graaf, depicted in figure 1. The aggregate production frontier TT' is "well behaved." If a community of identical individuals possessed the homothetic indifference curves I_1, I_2, I_3, then they would, at fixed market prices AA', choose either only x or only y and avoid the Pareto-optimal point M.

3. A further reason for the neglect of these pioneering efforts is perhaps that there was a considerable amount of argument between the two main figures, Farrell and Rothenberg. Fortunately, all the issues they argued about do not affect the substance of their analyses. Farrell, for example, digressed into the case where consumers maximized utility only locally. This subcase will be ignored in what follows. A more substantative argument lay in the use of aggregate indifference curves, which Farrell insisted could not be generally constructed and Rothenberg argued could be. As will be shown below, this is also a red herring because the pricing-out of Pareto-optimal allocations requires only the construction of *one* aggregate indifference curve, which both parties agree can be done. Finally, although Farrell, for example, asserted that the extension of the analysis from two to n dimensions was easy, there are a number of subtle points in the argument and some of Farrell's statements are misleading in their import.

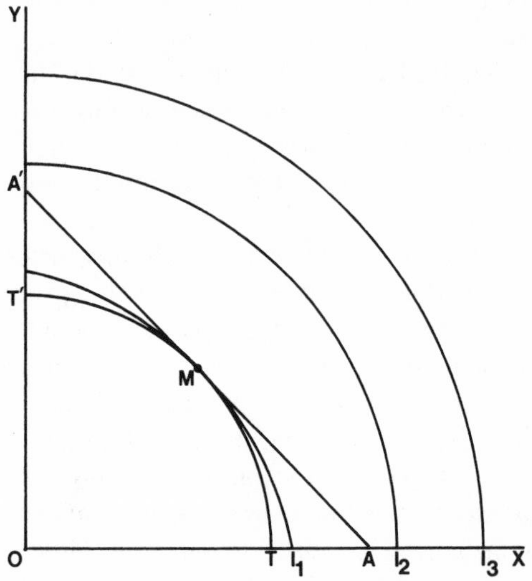

Figure 1. Pareto-optimality with a concave production frontier and concave social indifference curves.

It was Farrell's brilliant insight to observe that although the above argument was logically valid in the case of a single consumer, it was not necessarily correct in the case of a large community of identical individuals. Suppose, for example, that $AM = MA'$. Now, if one-half of the community chose A and the other half A', then the aggregate bundle chosen by society would be (a multiple of) M, and this is a feasible bundle. In general, the point M will divide AA' in proportions t and $1 - t$, and we need large numbers of individuals only to ensure that it makes sense for a proportion t of the community to choose A and for $1 - t$ to choose A'. For example, it sounds artificial to speak of 87/100ths of a community of four people choosing bundle A, but it makes perfectly good sense in a community of one hundred people. Rothenberg made the point clearly: "The effect of individual concavities . . . depends on whether the individual concavities impart non-convex constraints for the economy as a whole—that is, whether they entail aggregate concavities—or whether they 'cancel out' into over all convex constraints under aggregation" (1960:438).

Rothenberg's point is well made in his treatment of production nonconvexities. Suppose individual production frontiers look as shown in figure 2. If all firms are identical, then the aggregate production frontier will be as shown in figure 3, which indicates that the individual concavities look very small when compared with the size of the aggregate production possibilities. The more interesting case arises when all firms are not identical, so that the slope of lines like tt' are different across firms. The maximum amount of Y that can be produced, of course, occurs at M, where all firms

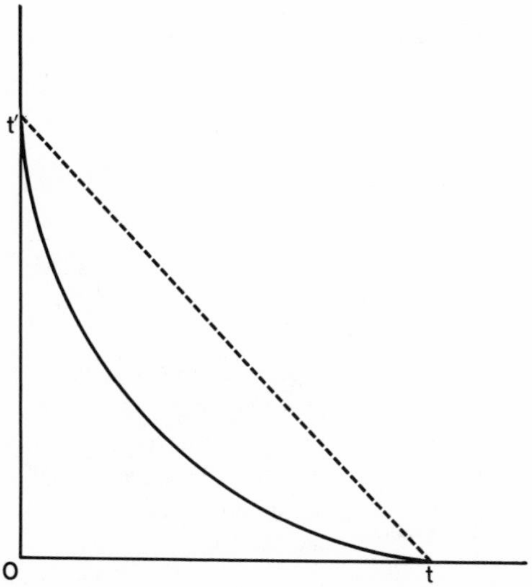

Figure 2. Fractional use of the end-points of the convex production set, which produces a linear frontier.

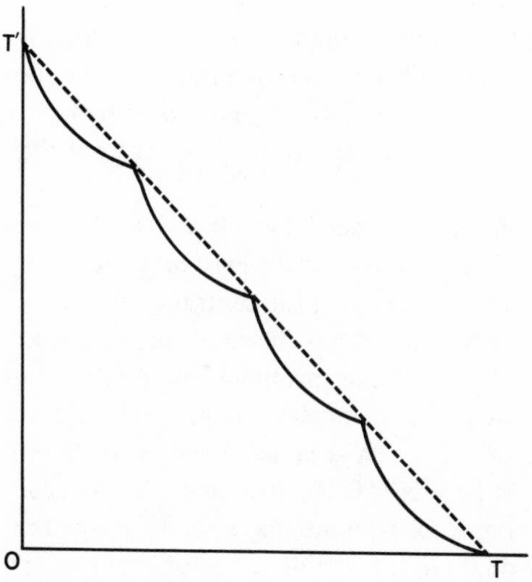

Figure 3. Approximate concavity of the aggregate production set when individual production sets are identical and nonconcave.

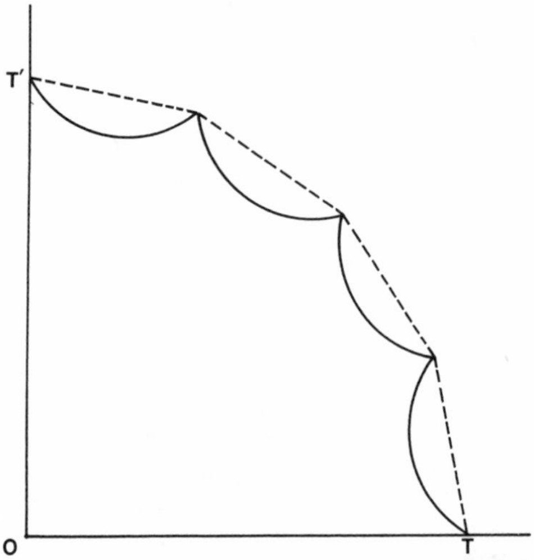

Figure 4. Approximate concavity of the aggregate production set when individual production sets are nonidentical and nonconcave.

produce Y; if we now wish to produce a little X, we will use that firm whose production frontier has the flattest slope; for the next increment of X we introduce the firm with a slightly steeper slope, and so on (figure 4). That the slopes become successively steeper readily establishes the approximate convexity of the aggregate production set. It is of fundamental importance that the convexity was obtained by using a simple economic argument—firms most efficient in the production of X should be used first, the next most efficient ones thereafter, and so on. Farrell and Rothenberg are clearly on solid ground. It remains only to clear up the loose ends of their analysis.[4]

At several places in their respective articles Farrell and Rothenberg make use of assumptions such as homotheticity or the existence of communities of identical individuals, without clarifying the centrality of such assumptions for their argument. Such assumptions, however, are not necessary. An analytical reformulation of the problem of pricing out Pareto-optimal allocations will show what is involved. Let there be T traders and n commodities and let $(X_1, \ldots, X_T)$ be a Tn vector of Pareto-optimal quantities. (The analysis here is restricted to an exchange economy for the sake of simplicity.) Let $P_t(X_t)$ denote the set of all points that are definitely preferred by individual t to the bundle actually given him. To

4. An alternative, and hitherto untried, route to the n-dimensional generalization would be to use a little-known paper by Kenneth Arrow (1952).

state that $(X_1, \ldots, X_T)$ is Pareto-optimal is equivalent to stating that no feasible rearrangement of commodity bundles exists which makes everyone better off. There do not exist $(y_1, \ldots, y_T)$ such that $y_t \in P_t(X_t)$, $t = 1, \ldots, T$ and $\Sigma y_t = \Sigma i_t$ where i_t is the bundle all individuals possess before trade takes place. This may be rewritten as there do not exist $(y_1, \ldots, y_T)$ such that,

$$\Sigma(y_t - i_t) = 0 \text{ and } (y_t - i_t) \in G_t(X_t), \text{ where } G_t = P_t(X_t) - i_t$$

or, that $\Sigma G_t \cap 0 = \emptyset$.

The last assertion follows because G_t indicates the preferred excess demand bundles, and if the aggregate preferred excess demands included 0, this would imply a feasible and preferred redistribution. The crux of the issue then is to find conditions under which ΣG_t is convex, because we can then draw a separating hyperplane between ΣG_t and 0 and thus price out the Pareto-optimal bundles.

The existence of a competitive equilibrium is a considerably more complicated mathematical question than the study of the Pareto-optimal allocations, but Farrell's conjecture on this issue may be illustrated by the following example. We begin with two consumers who have identical homothetic concave preferences, as shown in figure 5, each of whom begins at $I = (1, 1)$. Any price vector must, of course, pass through I and define a budget set such as BB'. A consumer will choose those points on a budget set that touch the highest feasible indifference curve. If the slope of

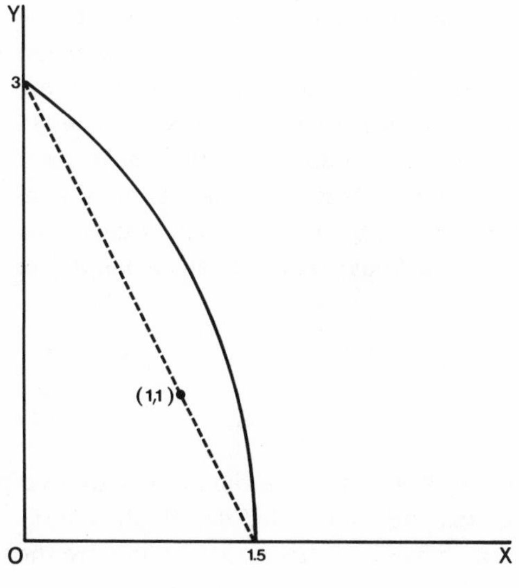

Figure 5. Individual optimality with concave indifference curves.

the price line is flatter than 2, each consumer will choose to buy only X; this decision will lead to an excess demand for X and an excess supply of Y, which is clearly not an equilibrium price vector. A symmetrical argument holds if the slope of the price line is steeper than 2. If there is an equilibrium, it must be reached by a price vector with slope 2. When the relative price is 2, each consumer has a choice of buying either 1.5 units of X or 3 units of Y. If both choose the same good, once again there can be no equilibrium. The final possibility is that individual A chooses X and individual B chooses Y. The aggregate demand vector is (1.5, 3). Aggregate supply is (2, 2), however, and the two are certainly not equal. Exactly the same analysis applies if A chooses Y and B chooses X. All possibilities have been exhausted, and it can now be claimed that there is no competitive equilibrium in this economy.

Suppose we now add a third identical individual, C, to this economy, thereby making aggregate supply equal to (3, 3). Once again, the only possibility for an equilibrium price vector is 2. This time, however, we have the possibility of letting A and B choose 1.5 units of X each while C chooses 3 units of Y. The total demand is now (3, 3), which exactly equals aggregate supply. So we do have a competitive equilibrium in the three-person economy.

As we add more identical traders to this economy, the following curious situation emerges. There is no equilibrium for four or five agents but an equilibrium for six; no equilibrium for seven or eight but an equilibrium for nine; and so on. If we have an economy with an arbitrarily large number N of agents, where N is not a multiple of 3, no equilibrium price vector exists. By adding or subtracting at most one trader, however, we can attain a competitive equilibrium. This result suggests that the distance of such an economy from equilibrium can be at most "one excess demand vector" in any economy; although this may be substantial when there are only a few agents, when there are ten thousand agents the excess demand of any one agent will be negligible when compared to the whole. As a result, we would conjecture that the extent of disequilibrium diminishes to zero as the number of agents grows without bound. This is the second part of Farrell's conjecture, and finding a rigorous proof of it will be the subject of chapter 7.

Edgeworth's Conjecture

The problem considered by Edgeworth is one of the simplest and yet most difficult in economics: when two individuals find it mutually advantageous to trade, such as a butcher bartering with a weaver, how are the terms at which the trade takes place settled? Turgot tacked this question in 1787 and realized that the solution was indeterminate—it all depended upon the bargaining abilities of the two individuals. No progress was made on this issue for more than a hundred years until Edgeworth undertook the problem. This situation is well represented by figure 6. Two individuals, A and B, start off with bundles $I_A = (x_A, y_A)$ and $I_B = (x_B, y_B)$ of goods x and y respectively. The total amount available to this two-person economy is shown in the figure as a box with dimensions $(x_a + x_B, y_A + y_B)$. O_A marks the origin for A and O_B the origin for B, so W denotes the initial allocation. The indifference curve A' represents the set of all commodity bundles that A considers indifferent to I_A; similarly for B'. If A and B decide to settle on any bundle in between A' and B', both will gain. But which point will they choose in this area? Suppose they pick V. We draw the curves A'' and B'' through V, corresponding to A' and B' through W. If there is an area enclosed between A'' and B'' (shaded in the figure), both individuals can gain by trading to some point within the shaded area. Mutual self-interest will put an end to trade only at those points where the indifference curves are mutually tangent, such as V'. The set of all points of mutual tangency, denoted CC', takes us as far as we can go in this situation. Two selfish and intelligent individuals will settle at some point on CC', but where?

Edgeworth made the brilliant observation that upon increasing the number of traders some of the indeterminacy is resolved. Suppose both A and B sprout identical twins so that although we have a four-person economy, it consists of two sets of identical twins. It is conceivable that in the two-person economy individual A, being a very poor bargainer, ends up at point D, where he is no better off than he was initially at W. In the four-person economy, however, it is plausible to think that individual A can

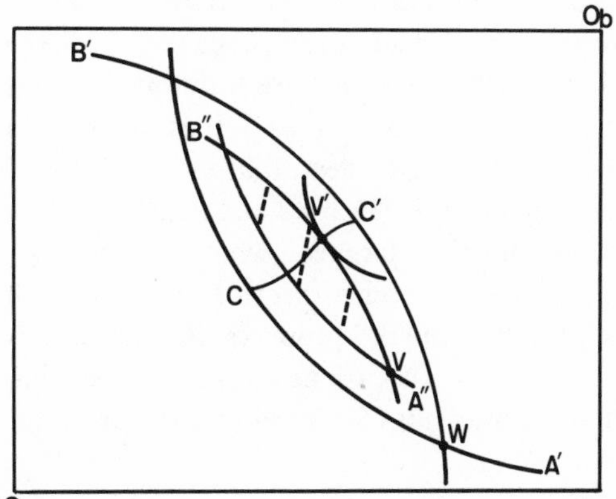

Figure 6. An Edgeworth box and its contract curve.

play off the B twins and make a better deal. As a result, some of the bargaining outcomes feasible in the two-person economy become infeasible in the four-person economy. As more twins are added, more bargaining solutions are eliminated. If we call the set of solutions obtained through bargaining the core of an economy, the process can be picturesquely expressed by saying that the core of an economy "shrinks" as the number of traders increases. It can be shown that the set of competitive equilibria always belongs to the core. Edgeworth conjectured that the core shrinks to precisely the competitive equilibria as the number of traders tends to infinity.

Edgeworth's conjecture is highly intuitive, but even a precise statement of the conjecture is by no means trivial. In our original economy, with individuals A_1 and B_1, an allocation of all goods was a four-dimensional vector $(X_{A1}, Y_{A1}, X_{B1}, Y_{B1})$. When the duplicates A_2 and B_2 are added, an allocation becomes $(X_{A1}, Y_{A1}, X_{B1}, Y_{B1}, X_{A2}, Y_{A2}, X_{B1}, Y_{B2})$, which is an eight-dimensional vector. If two more duplicates, A_3 and B_3, are added, the vector becomes 12-dimensional, and so on. As the dimension of the allocation vector increases, what is meant by saying that the core "shrinks"? How can a vector in twelve dimensions "shrink" to become a vector in four dimensions? If we can somehow "concentrate the action" in a space of fixed dimension, we can at least speak of the cores of larger economies, all of which will be subsets of the same fixed commodity space, as "shrinking" to the competitive equilibria. Furthermore, since everything would be happening in a space of fixed finite dimension, we could save ourselves the complications involved in formulating economies with an infinite number of agents. This is precisely what the brilliant and seminal paper of Gerard Debreu and Herbert Scarf succeeded in doing.

The idea of the Debreu-Scarf proof will be discussed later, but there are two points of special interest in their model. First, they let the size of the economy grow in a special way. We begin with a given economy ξ_N and then double it by adding to it an exact replica of itself. Call the new economy ξ_{2N}. We then enlarge ξ_{2N} by adding to it an exact replica of ξ_N, call the new economy ξ_{3N}, and so on. Essentially, then, we have N different agents with each agent having R duplicates of himself in ξ_{RN}. It is not true in general, even with this special way of adding traders, that identical agents must receive identical allocations in the core.[5] Debreu and Scarf therefore impose the condition of strict convexity of preferences, which ensures that, in replicated economies, identical agents receive identical allocations in the core. This is known as the "equal treatment" property. Because of this property, we can completely describe the allocations of ξ_{RN} by specifying only the bundles going to each of the N agents of different types, for exam-

5. See Green (1972).

ple, in ξ_{2N}, an allocation should be $(X_1, \ldots, X_N, X_{N+1}, \ldots, X_{2N})$, but if we assume agents 1 and $N + 1$ are identical, agents 2 and $N + 2$ are identical, and so on, the equal treatment property tells us that $X_1 = X_{N+1}$, $X_2 = X_{N+2}, \ldots$, and so on, and so we can unequivocally specify allocations by $(X_1, \ldots, X_N)$. By increasing the size of the economy through replication and imposing strict convexity of preferences Debreu and Scarf are able to prove Edgeworth's conjecture by staying within a space of fixed dimension.

The elegance of the Debreu-Scarf proof, however, depends crucially on the equal treatment property. Were it not that identical consumers get identical bundles in the core, the dimensionality of the allocation space would increase as the economy grew and the line of attack pursued above would fail. The proof of Edgeworth's conjecture poses new difficulties at this stage. The removal of the equal treatment property, for example, necessitates dealing with a sequence of economies in which the number of agents grows without bound. In the limit, this involves dealing with economies with a countable number of agents. Defining an allocation for such economies poses our first mathematical problem. If we define an allocation as

$$\lim_{N \to \infty} \left\{ \sum_R \sum_N X(t) = \sum_R \sum_N I(t) \right\}$$

or, equivalently,

$$\lim_{N \to \infty} \left\{ \sum_R \sum_N [X(t) - I(t)] \right\} = 0$$

then either the terms of $[X(t) - I(t)]$ have to be arbitrarily close to zero infinitely often, or, by an appropriate rearrangement, the infinite sum can be made to equal any arbitrary predetermined vector. This paradoxical result follows because the terms of the sequence $[X(t) - I(t)]$ will contain both positive and negative terms, and the convergence of such series, even in one dimension, is a considerable problem.[6] As a result, we are led to define allocations either as averages,

$$\lim_{N \to \infty} \frac{1}{RN} \sum_R \sum_N [X(t) - I(t)] = 0$$

or by some other procedure that will permit unambiguous definitions.

If we decide to define allocations in infinite economies by average equality of allocations with average equality of initial endowments, we will

6. This problem is explicitly noted by Werner Hildenbrand with reference to Scarf's original article of 1962: "The conceptual difficulty with this model is the definition of *attainable* allocation, i.e., to give meaning to the statement 'total demand equal total supply'" (1982:847).

be taking the measure-theoretic approach to large economies. So long as we have only the real numbers to work with there is little alternative to some such procedure. If, however, we have infinite numbers at our disposal, it should be just as straightforward to define feasible allocations in infinite economies as it was in finite ones. This is the nonstandard approach.

2

What Does Nonstandard Analysis Do?

Perhaps the worst enemy of nonstandard analysis has been its name. It is natural to suspect that a subject with such a name will be based on a logic that is *non*standard. Of course, the suspicion is entirely groundless. Nonstandard entities are only certain well-defined standard entities, and arguments involving such entities proceed entirely by standard means. At least as far as its acceptability is concerned, nonstandard analysis would have done better had it been called (more accurately) "an ultrapower model of analysis."

Nonstandard analysis is based on an embedding procedure, and the first half of this chapter seeks to show that this procedure is no more (or less) strange than other embeddings. The argument given here is meant to be persuasive and is principally directed at showing that there is nothing strange about nonstandard analysis—at least nothing stranger than the rest of mathematics. Chapter 3 then develops nonstandard analysis in a more rigorous fashion while trying to make it clear that mathematical logic is not needed to enable the use of nonstandard analysis. The two books I have found most helpful, especially in writing chapter 3, are those by J. M. Henle and E. M. Kleinberg (1979) and, at a more advanced level, by Martin Davis (1977). The best single volume for our purposes is by Albert E. Hurd and Peter A. Loeb (1985).

An Explanation of Nonstandard Analysis

The inspiration for nonstandard analysis arose from Leibniz's attempts to provide a rigorous foundation for the calculus in terms of infinitely small numbers, called infinitesimals. Everyone today is familiar with the concept of the derivate of a function $y = f(x)$ at the point x as

$$\frac{dy}{dx} = \lim_{\Delta x \to 0} \frac{f(x + \Delta x) - f(x)}{\Delta x}.$$

Geometrically, if y is a given point on a smooth curve $f(x)$ and $z, z', \ldots$ are a sequence of points on $f(x)$ tending to y, then we are approximating the slope of the tangent at x by the slope of nearby chords such as yz, yz', and so on. It is intuitively clear from this geometrical description that the slope of a chord ye, where e is infinitesimally close to y, would be infinitesimally close to the true slope. The existence of infinitesimals would thus circumvent the need for a limiting process and take us directly to an infinitely good approximation of the derivative. This at least was Leibniz's vision, but the infinitesimals, if they exist, cannot be found within the real numbers because the reals possess the following property, called the Archimedean property: If x and y are any two real numbers, then there exists an integer N such that $Nx > y$. No real number x can thus be infinitely small because a finite multiple of it, Nx, is greater than any given real number, y. In view of this difficulty Leibniz posited the existence of infinitely small numbers and asserted that they could be manipulated like ordinary real numbers.

The initial puzzle faced by students on hearing of nonstandard analysis is a visual one. They look at a straight line and try to imagine where the infinitely small numbers could find space to fit, but this is a thankless task because the real line displays no gaps where the infinitesimals could wait in ambush. Needless to say, our capacity to visualize is a victim of our habits. There are many mathematical entities that we take for granted because we were told about them before our critical faculties were fully aroused. Leopold Kronecker said that "God made the integers, Man made everything else," and there is no doubt that, historically, intelligent men have stumbled over concepts that schoolchildren today sail over, as, for example, the construction of the rationals from the integers.

A more difficult case is the transition from the rationals to the reals. It is commonly believed that the discovery that $\sqrt{2}$ was an irrational psychologically paralyzed Greek mathematicians because it attacked their mystical faith in integers as the only real entities. Their consternation can be appreciated by the following argument: Between any two rationals, there lies another rational, their average. Therefore, there cannot be a finite gap between two rationals, however small; or, stated differently, the rationals lie infinitely close to each other. But then where are the gaps the irrationals are supposed to fill? What is worse is that after accepting the existence of irrationals, it is subsequently proved that the totality of the irrationals is infinitely greater than the totality of the rationals. Visual inspection surely cannot reveal the gaps where these hordes of numbers are to fit. Indeed, because of the necessarily approximate nature of our measuring and drawing instruments we cannot even demonstrate the existence of a single irrational. We claim that we can approximate $\sqrt{2}$ as closely as we please, but the skeptic can easily retort that even our finest approximation involves an interval (a, b) and thus traps infinitely many rationals within our finest approximation. If we see the irrationals it is in the mind's eye. If we believe in their existence it is because they have arisen out of logical, not intuitive, necessity.

The last point is worth pursuing further. Take the case of the complex numbers. Nothing in our experience corresponds to the existence of $\sqrt{-1}$. Nonetheless, if we posit the existence of such numbers and derive certain simple rules for their manipulation, some remarkable properties follow. For example, every polynomial can be shown to possess a solution. The history of mathematics thus shows us repeatedly that concepts which were not intuitively demanded, or even plausible, have been systematically assimilated because their incorporation was shown to involve no inconsistency and because they provided us with new and interesting tools and theorems. Karel Hrbacek (1979) has provided a picturesque way of describing the situation with nonstandard numbers. They are to be visualized in the same manner that the class "birds" can be said to include not only all birds in existence but also birds that cannot now be seen such as the dodo and the phoenix. The example is especially illuminating in making us aware that we are to call "bird" not only those feathered creatures we see around us but also any animal that satisfies certain properties and whose existence does not involve us in a logical contradiction.

After this long harangue urging the acceptance of new concepts simply because they do not involve a contradiction, the reader may be surprised to find out that our next step is to exhibit "concretely" some nonstandard numbers, but a good general has to guard all fronts. A number x is said to be infinitely small compared to a number y if, when multiplied by an integer N, however large, $Nx < y$. We are all familiar with the order of words in a dictionary. By analogy we can define a lexicographic order on pairs of real numbers by the following rule $(a, b) > (c, d)$ if $a > c$, regardless of b and d. If $a = c$, $(a, b) > (c, d)$ if $b > d$. In this ordering, the first component fully determines which pair is greater, regardless of the value of the second component. Thus if $a > c$, then $(a, b) > (c, Nd))$, for all N. In other words, the contribution of the second component to the size of the pair is infinitely small. We can now claim that we have created infinitely small numbers, which will be pairs of the form $(0, x)$, while the usual real numbers are those of the form $(y, 0)$. The real difficulty in establishing

Leibniz's claim thus lies not in showing that infinitely small numbers exist but rather in showing that they can be manipulated exactly like ordinary numbers.

Although the lexicographic ordering provides us with suitable large and small numbers, it is unsatisfactory because we can never add up enough "infinitesimals" to get a real number—the gap between the reals and the infinitesimals is unbridgeable. So long as we stick with ordered pairs of finite length, there is no way of keeping the finite numbers and infinitesimals apart without using something akin to lexicographic ordering. We are, therefore, led to try out as our nonstandard numbers vectors of countably infinite length. It is well to begin by asking under what conditions we can expect to be completely successful.

Let us rehearse what it is that we wish to achieve: We want to embed the ordinary real numbers, R, in a larger structure, denoted by $^*R$, which will contain both infinitely large and infinitely small numbers, and we wish to have this embedding done in such a way that the entities of $^*R$ can, as far as possible, be manipulated exactly like the ordinary entities of R. Is this even possible? Suppose such an extension did exist. It would, of course, contain an entity $^*N$, corresponding to N, the nonnegative integers of R. Consider the following argument:

A. It is true that any well-defined subset of N has a least element. If all properties of N were true in $^*N$, the same would also be true of $^*N$.
B. Now $^*N \backslash N$, that is, the set of nonstandard integers that are not standard integers is a well-defined set.
C. If the principle described in A were to apply to $^*N \backslash N$, there would be a least integer in $^*N \backslash N$, call it υ.
D. But then $\upsilon - 1$ must belong to N.
E. If $\upsilon - 1$ belongs to N, $(\upsilon - 1) + 1\ (= \upsilon)$ belongs to N, since the successor of any integer is also in N.
F. υ belongs to both N and $^*N \backslash N$, which is a contradiction.

This example shows us that if we wish to obtain a consistent extension of R, we cannot permit arbitrary subsets of $^*R$ to be well-defined. To see which subsets have to be avoided, as well as to see how little is lost by such a qualification, the structure $^*R$ has to be built carefully. To begin with, let us simply construct an extension that contains infinitely large and infinitely small numbers and is also open to some manipulation like R and then fill in the details of the entire construction.

We now define nonstandard numbers as infinite sequences of the form $(x_1, x_2, \ldots, x_n, \ldots)$. The real numbers are naturally embedded in this framework by means of the constant sequences, for example, $4 = (4,$

4, . . . , 4, . . .). Now consider the sequence (1, 2, 3, 4, . . . , n, . . .) which we denote by ω. This sequence is greater than any integer N in an infinity of components (actually, it is less than N only on a finite number of places) and may properly be considered an infinite integer. Similarly, we can see that $\epsilon = (1, 1/2, 1/3, \ldots, 1/n, \ldots)$ should be considered as smaller than any real number. Furthermore, if we define the multiplication of such numbers pointwise, we have $\epsilon\omega = (1, 1, \ldots, 1, \ldots) = 1$. Not only have we obtained infinitely larger and infinitely small numbers by means of this construction, but we have also obtained the result that an infinitesimal added up an infinitely large number of times gives us a real number, exactly as desired.

In considering ω an infinite number, we have disregarded the fact that ω was less than any given integer N on a finite number of components. If we are to obtain a proper extension of the real numbers, it is essential that we disregard what happens on a finite number of components, otherwise—sequences such as (2, 1, 3, 3, 3, . . . , 3, . . .) and (1, 2, 3, 3, 3, . . . , 3, . . .) would be incomparable and our extended "Leibniz numbers" would not possess a property true of the real numbers—that is, for all real numbers r_1, r_2, either $r_1 \geq r_2$ or $r_1 < r_2$.

We could, as a first try, define two nonstandard numbers to be equal if they agree, pointwise, on the complement of a finite set. Thus two nonstandard numbers, $a = [a(j)]$ and $b = [b(j)]$, are equal if and only if the set of indices j for which $a(j) = b(j)$ is the complement of a finite set. This construction, however, suffers from the defect that we may be unable to assign any value to some infinite sequences, for example (1, 2, 1, 2, 1, 2, . . .). This sequence should be either 1 or 2, but it cannot be either because it differs from both 1 and 2 an infinity of times. Using the family of subsets consisting of the complements of finite sets will thus leave gaps in our extended number system. We are looking for a class of subsets, U, of the countable sets, N, such that, for any subset A of N, either A is in U or the complement of A, denoted N/A, is in U. This property may be called maximality.

Two further conditions are necessary for consistency. If $A \in U$ and $B \supseteq A$, then we must have $B \in U$ as well; otherwise by maximality of U, $N/B \in U$. Define a sequence equal to 1 on A and 0 on N/B. This sequence can be neither 0 nor 1, and we have a sequence that does not define a "Leibniz number." Now consider $A \in U$, $B \in U$ but $A \cap B \notin U$. Define a sequence to be 1 on A/B and 0 on B/A. Once again we cannot assign a value to this sequence, and so we must require $A \cap B \in U$. Alternatively, we may motivate these conditions as follows: Consider two sequences, ϕ and γ, with $\phi(i) = 2$ on A and $\gamma(i) = 3$ on B. Then we would like to say $\phi < \gamma$ and hence we want $B \in U$. Now suppose $\phi < \gamma$ and $\gamma < \rho$ and let $A =$

$[i \mid \phi(i) < \gamma(i)]$, $B = [i \mid \gamma(i) < \rho(i)]$, then $A \cap B \subset [i \mid \phi(i) < \rho(i)]$. Hence, if we want $\phi < \rho$, then requiring that $A \cap B \in U$ will be sufficient.

Gathering together all our strands, we are looking for a collection of subsets, U, of the countable set, N, which is such that

1. $\phi \notin U$ (ϕ denotes the empty set).
2. If $A \in U$, $B \in U$, then $A \cap B \in U$.
3. If $A \in U$, and $B \in P(N)$, the set of all subsets of N, with $A \subseteq B$, then $B \in U$.
4. If $B \in P(N)$, then either $B \in U$ or $N/B \in U$.
5. No finite subset of N is an element of U.

Such a family of subsets of N is called a *free ultrafilter* on N. (The existence of free ultrafilters is proved by using the axiom of choice.) By defining nonstandard numbers according to the procedure outlined above, and using the free ultrafilter whose existence can be guaranteed, we can construct a proper extension $^*R$ of the real numbers, R. This construction was originated by Abraham Robinson (1965), who also showed that any property of the real numbers that could be written down in a formal language would be true of $^*R$ if it was true for R. The construction described above is known as the ultrapower construction, and we have intuitively shown that a suitable ultrapower of the real numbers, R, will provide us with the nonstandard numbers, $^*R$.

Once students have been convinced that infinitesimals are as legitimate as irrationals or complex numbers they are anxious to use the new concepts immediately. It is therefore an unpleasant shock for them to find that they cannot manipulate all nonstandard concepts exactly like standard ones, but only the *internal* nonstandard entities. The existence of noninternal, or *external*, nonstandard concepts, which are not necessarily subject to the normal rules of mathematics, tends to lead some students to throw up their hands in despair. This would be a mistake for two reasons. First, by a consideration of the rationals and the integers it may be shown that we do not apply exactly the same principles to the rationals, which we might well label "nonstandard integers," as we do to the integers. Nonetheless, it took us very little time in grade school to recognize this difference and modify our reasonings accordingly. Second, and this is a bribe, readers who are willing to bear with us through the concept "external" will find us harassing their intuition no further. Hereafter, we can get to work.

Let Q denote the rationals and N the integers. We can add, subtract, and multiply the integers and, given any nonempty subset of the integers, we can always find a first element. Although we can also add, subtract, and multiply the rationals, it is no longer true that every nonempty subset necessarily has a first element. Consider the collection of all rationals greater than 0. This is a nonempty set, but it has no first element; if x is proposed as a first element, $x/2$ is smaller than x and positive. So we reach a contradiction.

This simple example shows us that when we enlarge our original set of integers, N, to obtain the rationals, Q, we must recognize the possibility of creating sets in Q that do not obey all the rules of sets in N. Any function $f(x)$ can be viewed as the set of two-tuples which satisfy $[(x, y) \mid y = f(x)]$. Therefore any qualification that we apply to sets must also apply to functions and from thence to sets of sets or functions of functions and so on until it infects all the entities used in analysis. An external concept is therefore simply one that does not necessarily obey all the rules of the original structure.

It is important to remind ourselves that external notions do not hinder our normal thinking once we become used to them, and, so to speak, absorb their existence. Indeed, most of the time we are not even aware of the shift between N and Q. It is equally important to remember that results *about* a structure need not be obtained *within* the structure itself. The complex numbers, for example, do not possess many of the properties of the integers but, nonetheless, deep and powerful theorems about the integers have been proved using complex numbers; this is the work of the branch of mathematics called analytic number theory. In much the same way, we shall be using nonstandard methods to prove results about the standard world.

The ultrafilter construction shown earlier gave us a way of looking at the nonstandard integers $^*N$. These contain all of N, but in addition they include integers in $^*N - N$, such as ω. Since all the integers N can be ordered by size and since $^*N$ is the nonstandard counterpart of N, it follows that all the rules of N apply to $^*N$. As noted earlier, the set N is an external subset of $^*N$. To see this important point yet again, suppose N were internal, that is, a "good" set in the nonstandard framework, and we could apply ordinary reasoning to it. Then N is a nonempty set of integers which is bounded above (any $\omega \in {}^*N - N$ is a bound for N); it must therefore possess a largest element M. But if $M \in N$, $M + 1 \in N$ and $M + 1 > M$; so we have a contradiction.

If N is an external subset, then any function whose definition involves N specifically is external and could be badly behaved. The following example shows that this is indeed so. It is well known that, for all integers $n \in N$, if the domain of a function has less than n elements, the function must attain its maximum. If we are to transfer this statement, it should be true that, for all $n \in {}^*N$, if a function has domain of cardinality less than n, the function must have a maximum. We will show that this is false for external functions. Let $\omega \in {}^*N - N$, where $^*N$ is the nonstandard extension of the positive integers. Define $f(n) = 1 - 1/n$ for all $n \in N$ and $f(n) = 0$ for all $n \in {}^*N \leq \omega$. f clearly does not achieve its maximum, 1. The difficulty with the function f above is that it could not have been written as a sentence of the language L. Properties of R which are true in $^*R$ must be expressible as sentences of L, and the property of being thus expressible is called internal. Even though the property of being expressible as a sentence in a formal language is not a very intuitive one, it is nonetheless possible, with a little practice, to decide whether a function is internal or not.

Because external entities are best avoided while proving theorems, it is unsatisfactory to say, "Practice will tell you how to recognize them"—this is dangerously close to "When you are wrong, you have used something external." Chapter 3 will deal with this issue more formally. The two examples given above do, however, convey the essence of the problem, and a very good rule of thumb for all the problems we shall be concerned with is to beware of concepts that involve countable elements or operations.

Appendix: A Historical Digression

It sometimes happens that the very success of a particular formulation of a problem militates against new ideas and fresh developments. Modern analysis has arisen out of the method of limits, and the very success of modern analysis makes us forget all the doubts and uncertainties that had to be faced before this magnificent structure could be raised. The method of limits was not, however, the method by which the calculus, the backbone of analysis, was raised—infinitesimals were the actual tools employed. To make the use of nonstandard analysis more plausible it may be useful to remind the reader of two facts from the history of mathematics. First, infinitely large quantities are not new; what is new is the capacity of our new methods to manipulate these entities. Second, the early history of the calculus is riddled with attempts to formulate a successful way of handling infinitesimals.

I. In *100 Years of Mathematics* George Temple (1981:19–25) shows that infinitely large quantities were defined and developed by such mathematicians as Guiseppe Veronese in 1891, Otto Hölder in 1910, Arthur Moritz Schönflies in 1906, Tullio Levi-Civita in 1892, David Hilbert in 1899, Paul Bois-Reymond in 1882, Godfrey Harold Hardy in 1910, Hans Hahn in 1907, and Thoralf Skolem in 1929. This list of eminent names may persuade one that infinite quantities have a history, but one may wonder whether such entities can arise in any simple fashion. The two following examples are adapted from Friedrich Waismann's *Introduction to Mathematical Thinking* (1951).

1. Consider the family of functions $y^\alpha = 1/x^\alpha$. Each of these functions goes to infinity as x goes to zero. Nonetheless, by considering the ratio $y^{\alpha_1}/y^{\alpha_2} = x^{\alpha_2 - \alpha_1} > 1$, whenever $\alpha_1 > \alpha_2$, it seems self-evident to assert that the functions y^α tend to infinity faster as α increases. We can now use α as a numerical index for the speed with which y^α goes to infinity. This indexing exhausts all the positive real numbers. If the function $y = |\log x|$ is now considered, by taking a Taylor series expansion, it becomes obvious that $|\log x|$ has a slower rate of increase than any of the functions y^α. So we have to speak of $|\log x|$ going to infinity at an infinitely slower rate than any y^α, if we are to be consistent. But then $|\log x|$ goes to infinity at a rate that is positive, yet smaller than any real number.

The second example is a modification of the horn-shaped angles known to antiquity. Consider the angle formed by a straight line and a circle tangent to this line. Now draw several more circles, all of which are tangent to the straight line and have the same point of tangency, Z (figure 7). If γ is the radius of the circle, we can set $1/\gamma = \omega$ as the magnitude of the "angle" closed between the straight line and the circle. The sequence $\omega, 2\omega, 3\omega, \ldots$ forms an ever-increasing sequence of angles as we draw circles with smaller and smaller radii. Nonetheless, no member of this sequence will ever equal *any* straight line angle such as α drawn at Z.

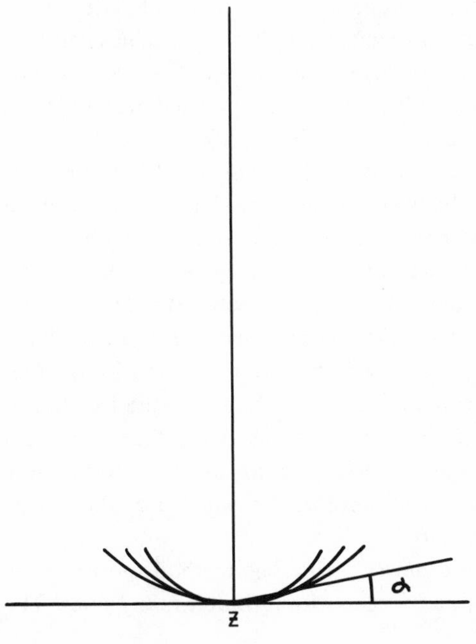

Figure 7. Infinite and finite illustrated by the relationship between angles.

In other words, α is infinitely larger than any of the curvilinear angles such as ω.

It would seem that infinite entities are fairly easy to find once we are willing to search for them.

II. The use of infinitesimals in developing the calculus can be appreciated by taking a simple problem with an ancient history (Waismann, 1951:220–23). Consider two circles with radii R and r respectively. How can we form an idea of the ratio of their areas? By inscribing similar polygons within each circle it is seen that no matter how many sides each polygon has the ratio of the areas of the two similar polygons is always as the ratio $R^2:r^2$. This naturally leads the imagination to conceive of a polygon with so many sides that it covers the circle infinitely finely. In this case, the areas of the polygons are still as $R^2:r^2$, so it is natural to conclude that $R^2:r^2$ must be the ratio of the areas themselves. This last step requires us to accept the claim that "a circle is nothing but a polygon with infinitely many sides." The ancients were unwilling to consider this last as an axiom. So they developed the method of *reductio ad absurdum*, which involves two steps: first, we assume that the ratio of the area is as $R^2:\bar{r}^2$ where $\bar{r} > r$ and show that this leads to a contradiction; second, we assume that the ratio is as $R^2:\bar{\bar{r}}^2$, with $\bar{\bar{r}} < r$, and show that this too leads to a contradiction. We conclude, then, that the areas of the two circles must be in the ratio $R^2:r^2$. This method is very clear, but it has the disadvantage of being cumbersome. Furthermore, the method of proof is different from the intuition that guided us to the result. This discrepancy was an irritant to later mathematicians, and it led John Wallis to wonder whether Archimedes had purposely "covered up the trails of his investigations, as if he has grudged posterity the secret of his method of inquiry, while he wished to extort from them the assent of his results" (Edwards, 1979:29–30).

Archimedes did write another treatise explaining his intuitive process, but it was not discovered until the twentieth century. The treatise is called *The Method*, and it is pleasant to note that the secret of Archimedes' method amounts exactly to the assumption that "a circle is nothing but a polygon with infinitely many sides" (Edwards, 1979:68–71). This treatise was, of course, unknown to Kepler, who seems to have been repelled by the distinction between obtaining a result and obtaining its proof. In his treatise on the solid geometry of wine barrels Johan Kepler made free use of infinitesimal reasoning and justified himself by asserting that "we could obtain absolute and in all respects perfect demonstrations from these books of Archimedes themselves, [sic] were we not repelled by the thorny reading thereof" (Edwards, 1979:103).

It would be nice if we could devise a rigorous method to justify the belief that a circle is nothing but a polygon with infinitely many sides. The early history of the calculus provides two such efforts, by Bonaventura Cavalieri and by Blaise Pascal. Cavalieri followed the lead of Kepler and popularized the systematic use of indivisibles by arguing that any geometrical figure was made up of infinitely many figures of lower dimension. Thus, a square was made up of infinitely many lines and a line consisted of infinitely many points. This would not be such a problem if it was not simultaneously added that a point has no length at all. A later mathematician plaintively demands: "How many nothings, then, does it take to make something? Who can tell us? The demand is too much for the human mind" (Bledsoe, 1868:57).

To avoid this paradox, Pascal continued to use the term "indivisibles" but would approximate a plane figure by using only finite rectangles, thereby avoiding all dimensionality problems. How, then, could he make a circle equal its approximating rectangles? Pascal introduced a new postulate to the effect that if two finite quantities "differ from each other by an indefinitely small quantity," then "the one may be taken for the other without making the slightest difference in the result." This is another way of reintroducing infinitesimals, and the incorporation of such logic led to assertions of the form "$a + dx + dx^2 = a$" in dictionaries of mathematics (Davies and Peck, *Dictionary of Mathematics*, quoted in Bledsoe, 1868:64).

One must admire the philosophical resolve of the generations of mathematicians who continued to use the calculus because of its inordinate utility while having to gulp when faced with simple queries about the nature of the objects they worked with. The biographies of Cambridge students of the early nineteenth century make it clear that they had trouble accepting their doses of mathematics. Even as late as 1855 a mathematician of the caliber of Isaac Todhunter offered the following explanation to troubled students:

> A difficulty of a more serious kind, which is connected with the notion of a limit, appears to embarrass many students of this subject—namely, a suspicion that the methods employed are only approximately, and therefore a doubt as to whether the results are absolutely, true. This objection is certainly very natural, but at the same time by no means easy to meet, on account of the inability of the reader to point out any indefinite place at which his uncertainty commences. In such a case all he can do is to fix his attention very carefully on some part of the subject, as the theory of expansions for example, where specific important formulas are obtained. He must examine the demonstrations, and if he can find a flaw in them, he must allow that results *absolutely true and free from all approximation* can be legitimately derived by the doctrine of limits. (Quoted in Bledsoe, 1868:71)

Even this slight sketch of the historical doubts and uncertainties that have beset the calculus suggests that claims of the self-sufficiency of the method of limits leans heavily on the old English adage

Treason doth never prosper.
What's the reason?
If it does prosper,
None dare call it treason.

The success of the method of limits has been enormous, and its reputation is eminently deserved, but should it now raise itself as a bar to further development?

3

A More Detailed Look at Nonstandard Analysis

Defining the Superstructure

It is convenient to begin by recalling that the nonstandard numbers introduced earlier were actually functions from the index set N to the real numbers R, that is, $*r \in *R$ implies $*r: N \to R$. If we are given an arbitrary set S instead of R we can still mimic our earlier construction. For every $s \in S$, we could define the set $*S$ as the (equivalence class) of the set of mappings from N to S. All elements $s \in S$ would be embedded in $*S$ by means of the constant mappings $(s, s, \ldots, s, \ldots)$. $*S$ would thus contain S, and if S, for example, consists of a countable number of distinct elements $s_1, s_2, \ldots, s_n, \ldots$, then the element of $*S$ denoted by $\rho = (s_1, s_2, \ldots, s_n, \ldots)$ would certainly be different from each s_i and $*S$ would contain an element different from every element of S.

The above construction, whereby the new entities are simply functions with the index set as domain, can obviously be conducted for any set, and we can define the new entities unambiguously by using the ultrafilter. If we can find a set $\mathbf{X}$ large enough (and complicated enough) to include "all of standard analysis," then the ultrapower based on this set will give us a model of nonstandard analysis.

To obtain such a magnificent $\mathbf{X}$, define the following sets inductively:

$$X_0 = R$$

$$\vdots$$

$$X_{n+1} = P\left(\bigcup_{k=0}^{n} X_k\right), \qquad n = 0, 1, 2, \ldots$$

where $P(Z)$ denotes the power set of Z—that is, the set of all subsets of Z. Now we define a new set $\mathbb{X}$ by means of the following formula:

$$\mathbb{X} = \bigcup_{n=0}^{\infty} X_n .$$

The object $\mathbb{X}$ thus constructed is called a superstructure. That $\mathbb{X}$ is adequate for defining all objects of interest in standard analysis may be seen as follows:

We chose as X_0 the real numbers, R. Therefore, X_1 will contain all subsets of R, X_2 will contain all Cartesian products and in particular all functions; higher-order X_i will include all functions of functions, and so on, and we can go on to include any object of interest in standard analysis. Algebraic operations on X_0 are also included with $\mathbb{X}$, as may be seen by using the following entities for sum, product, and less than:

$$S = [(a, b, c): a, b, c \in X_0 \text{ and } a + b = c]$$

$$P = [(a, b, c): a, b, c \in X_0 \text{ and } a \cdot b = c]$$

$$L = [(a, b): a, b \in X_0 \text{ and } a \leq b].$$

We may therefore claim that the superstructure $\mathbb{X}$ based on R, the real numbers, contains all of standard analysis.

We now form $*X$, an ultrafilter model of $\mathbb{X}$. This ultrafilter model will be based on $*R$, which is a proper extension of the real numbers and will allow us to perform all the operations of standard analysis. The one point that we have to be careful about is that every nonstandard entity be defined by a map whose range is contained in some X_n; however large n may be, there must be a bound to it. Otherwise, the entity ξ defined by $\xi(\nu) \in X_\nu \backslash X_{\nu-1}$ would not be a number, a function, a function of a function, and so forth. Indeed, ξ would have no counterpart in all of standard analysis. With this one caution, we may now claim that we have formed a nonstandard model for analysis. The details of this construction may be found in Stroyan and Luxemburg (1976).

The theorem that will be vital for our purposes will state: *Any property of* $\mathbb{X}$ *that can be expressed as a sentence with bounded quantifiers in a formal language is true for* $\mathbb{X}$ *if and only if it is also true for* $*\mathbb{X}$. To be able to use this result we will have to learn how to write out sentences in formal languages. (This is *not* the same as learning mathematical logic.)

Setting Up the Language

A *formal language* $\mathcal{L}$ consists of a set $\mathcal{A}$, called the *alphabet* of $\mathcal{L}$. The members of $\mathcal{A}$ are called *symbols*. $\mathcal{A}$ consists of the union of three pairwise disjoint sets:

$$\mathcal{A} = \mathcal{A}_1 \cup \mathcal{A}_2 \cup \mathcal{A}_3.$$

The symbols belonging to $\mathcal{A}_1$ are denoted below together with their meanings on the right.

$=$ equality
$\in$ belongs to
$\neg$ not
& and
$\exists$ there exists
$\forall$ for all
V or
$\rightarrow$ implies
( ) brackets for separation of symbols
$\langle\ \rangle$ brackets for denoting ordered pairs

The symbols that belong to $\mathcal{A}_2$ form a countably infinite set and are called *variables*.

The set $\mathcal{A}_3$ consists of the names of the objects we wish to talk about. It thus differs from $\mathcal{A}_1$ and $\mathcal{A}_2$ in that its composition will depend upon the particular universe we wish to discuss. The symbols of $\mathcal{A}_3$ are known as the constants of $\mathcal{L}$, and since we may wish to talk about arbitrary sets, the cardinality of $\mathcal{A}_3$ is arbitrary. When we have two different languages, $\mathcal{L}$ and $^*\mathcal{L}$, then $\mathcal{A}_1$ and $\mathcal{A}_2$ will generally be common to both languages, which will differ only by $\mathcal{A}_3$.

As is the case in any language, certain strings of symbols make no sense, such as

$$)(\& \quad \text{or} \quad \neg\in\exists.$$

Logicians have devised rules to avoid such nonsense, but since our aim is not to learn logic we will simply trust the reader to recognize (and write) strings of symbols that can be interpreted. Thus, if we are talking about integers and we wish to say that an ordering relation "greater than," denoted $>$, exists between all pairs of numbers, then we would write the following:

$$(\forall x_1)(\forall x_2)((x_1 > x_2) \vee (x_1 = x_2) \vee (x_2 > x_1)).$$

In words, this says, "For all x_1 and for all x_2 in the domain, (the real numbers), one of the following statements is true: either x_1 is larger than x_2, or x_1 equals x_2 or x_2 is larger than x_1." Of all the statements that do make sense, however, some cannot be interpreted as unambiguously true or false. For example, in the case of the integers,

$$x > 4$$

can be both true or false, depending upon the value of x. The meaning of the above statement is free to vary with x, which is said to have a free occurrence. We do not want our symbols to take liberties with us, so we will focus on those statements where the interpretation of x is bound by a quantifier, $\forall$ or $\exists$. Such statements, in which every occurrence of a variable is bound by a quantifier, is called a *sentence*. In the example above, if we said, $(\exists x)(x > 4)$—there exists an integer greater than 4—we would have made a true sentence. If, however, we had said, $(\forall x)(x > 4)$—all integers are greater than 4—we would have made a false sentence. In either case, the point is that we would have made a claim that could be unambiguously decided.

The Transfer Principle

We are concerned with only two mathematical structures, $\mathbf{X}$ and $^*\mathbf{X}$. Let $\mathfrak{L}$ and $^*\mathfrak{L}$ denote two formal languages, meant to talk about $\mathbf{X}$ and $^*\mathbf{X}$ respectively. If a sentence α of $\mathfrak{L}$ is true in $\mathbf{X}$ we write $\mathfrak{F}\alpha$. If a sentence β of $^*\mathfrak{L}$ is true in $^*\mathbf{X}$ we write $^*\mathfrak{F}\beta$. We wish to relate $\mathfrak{F}$ to $^*\mathfrak{F}$.

Consider a sentence α of $\mathfrak{L}$. Suppose it contains a constant c. This c is the name of some entity ξ in $\mathbf{X}$. Since $\mathbf{X}$ is embedded in $^*\mathbf{X}$, there must be an element $^*\xi \in {}^*\mathbf{X}$ which arises out of ξ through the ultrafilter construction. Because $^*\mathfrak{L}$ is a language for $^*\mathbf{X}$ it must contain a name $^*c$ for $^*\xi$. Similarly, every constant of α in $\mathfrak{L}$ has a corresponding replacement in $^*\mathfrak{L}$. Replace every constant c by its corresponding $^*c$. The sentence $^*\mathfrak{L}$ thus obtained is denoted by $^*\alpha$. We can now state the transfer principle: Let α be a sentence of $\mathfrak{L}$. Then,

$$^*\mathfrak{F}\,^*\alpha \text{ if and only if } \mathfrak{F}\alpha.$$

The transfer principle is a very important tool, but it is only a tool. To take an analogy, it is easy to write down a transfer principle that converts arabic numerals into roman numerals, but it is doubtful whether anything worthwhile about either number system can be learned by such a principle.

To illustrate the transfer principle, let us consider the following sentence of $\mathcal{L}$, which expresses the Archimedean property of the real number system:

$$\mathfrak{F}(\forall x \in R)(\exists n \in N)(x < n).$$

This sentence tells us that, given any real number x, there exists an integer n greater than x. The transferred statement says

$$*\mathfrak{F}(\forall x \in *R)(\exists n \in *N)(x < n).$$

The transferred statement tells us that "for any nonstandard real number, there exists a nonstandard integer larger than it." In other words, $*R$ is *Archimedean. This is not the same as telling us that "there exists a nonstandard integer larger than any real number." (Compare carefully the two sentences in quotation marks.) To obtain this (interesting) conclusion we have to do a little work and cannot simply transfer. I showed earlier that there existed a nonstandard integer ω such that $\omega > n$ for all $n \in N$. By the Archimedean axiom, for any $r \in R$, there exists $n \in N$ such that $r < n$. Combining the two statements, we have

for all $r \in R$, $\omega > r$.

Our conclusion can be expressed by saying that:

There exists a nonstandard integer ω larger than
any real number.

This statement refers to a nonstandard integer and is certainly not in $\mathcal{L}$. But because it refers to R (and not $*R$), it is not a statement in $*\mathcal{L}$ either. *It is an external statement and a true one*. By the same token, the statement that

"$\epsilon = 1/\omega$ is an infinitesimally small number, that is,
a nonzero number smaller than any real number,"

is both true and external. Most of the interesting results proved in this book are of this nature. Examples illustrating this point are provided below after some preliminaries on notation and orderings on $*R$.

Using Nonstandard Analysis

I stated earlier that $*\mathfrak{X}$ is a structure which is built on $\mathfrak{X}$ and which inherits all properties of $\mathfrak{X}$ that can be written down in formal sentences with bounded quantifiers. Since $\mathfrak{X}$ has R, $*\mathfrak{X}$ has the extension $*R$; $\mathfrak{X}$ has sets $S \subseteq R^n$ and functions $f: R^n \to R$ hence $*\mathfrak{X}$ has extensions $*S \subseteq *R^n$

and $^*f : {}^*R^n \to R$ such that the properties of f and S are inherited by $^*f$ and $^*S$. Taking $|\cdot|$, the absolute value function, as an example, for $^*x \in {}^*R$, $^*|\cdot|$ is defined by

$$^*|^*x| = \begin{cases} ^*x & \text{if} \quad ^*x \; ^*\geq \; ^*0 \\ -^*x & \text{if} \quad ^*x \; ^*< \; ^*0 \end{cases}$$

because this is how the definition of $|\cdot|$ would be written in $\mathcal{L}$.

It will be seen that the above notation is exceptionally clumsy, and our meaning could be more clearly (and cleanly) expressed by dropping the * on 0 since the zero of R and $^*R$ are the same (R is embedded within $^*R$) and the * on $^*\geq$ and $^*<$ since these relations are just the extensions of $\geq$ and $<$. In the same vein it is customary to drop * from all basic entities whenever the meaning is evident from the context. For $x, y \in {}^*R$ we will simply write $x + y$ for the sum instead of $x \; ^*\!+ \; y$, and so forth. The extension of $|\cdot|$, in the new notation, is given by, $\forall x \in {}^*R$,

$$^*|\;| = \begin{cases} x & \text{if} \quad x \geq 0 \\ -x & \text{if} \quad x < 0 \end{cases}$$

Once the definition of $^*|\cdot|$ is clear, we will even drop the * from it and refer simply to $|x|$ for $x \in {}^*R$.

We can also divide the class of internal functions into those that arise as the nonstandard extension of some standard function and those that do not arise in this fashion; for example, $^*f(x) = x$, $0 \leq x \leq 1$, is the nonstandard extension of $f(x) = x$, $0 \leq x \leq 1$. Note that the domain of $^*f$ includes points not in $[0, 1]$—it includes values in $^*R$ which are infinitesimally close to zero, denoted by $\epsilon \simeq 0$.

If we now define $^*g(x) = x$, $\epsilon \leq x \leq 1$, $\epsilon \simeq 0$, we obtain an internal function which is not the extension of any standard function, because the domain $\epsilon \leq x \leq 1$ is not the extension of any domain in the standard world.

Similarly, the function $^*h(x) = \log x$, $1 \leq x \leq 10$ is the nonstandard extension of the standard function $h(x) = \log x$, $1 \leq x \leq 10$, and the functions $^*j(x) = \log x$, $1 \leq x \leq \omega$, $\omega \in {}^*N - N$ or

$$^*k(x) = \frac{\log x}{\omega}, \qquad 1 \leq x \leq 100, \qquad \omega \in {}^*N - N$$

are both internal nonstandard functions that do not arise as the extension of standard functions.

Because R is an ordered field it follows that $^*R$ will also be an ordered field. If $^*r \in {}^*R$ is finite in the usual sense, that is, $|^*r| < n$, for some $n \in N$, then there exists a unique real number which is infinitesimally close to

$^*r$. We denote this unique real number by $°r$, the *standard part* of $^*r$. Those nonstandard numbers whose standard part is zero are known as the *infinitesimals*. If ϵ is an infinitesimal, so is $-\epsilon$. The distance between $^*r$ and $°r$ is infinitesimal, denoted $\simeq$, $^*r \simeq r$, or, equivalently, if we remember that infinitesimals can be both positive and negative, $^*r - °r \simeq 0$. For any $r \in R$, the *monad* of r is the set:

$$\text{monad}\,(r) = \{x \in {}^*R : x \simeq r\}.$$

If we can imagine ourselves in possession of a microscope capable of viewing infinitesimals, figure 8 is often useful.

A real sequence $(S_n)_{n \in N}$ is a function $S: N \to R$. It therefore has a nonstandard extension $^*S: {}^*N \to {}^*R$, denoted $(S_n)_{n \in {}^*N}$. Since the statement $S(n) = S_n$ is true in $\mathbf{X}$ it is true in $^*\mathbf{X}$. It follows that $^*S_n = S_n$ for all $n \in N$, that is, $^*S_n$ is identical with S_n for all standard integers n. For simplicity of notation, write $^*S_n = S_n$ even for $n \in {}^*N - N$.

THEOREM 1. $S_n \to S$ *if and only if* $^*S_n \approx S$ *for all infinite* $n \in {}^*N - N$.

Note that the statement of the theorem involves the external concept $\approx$ or "infinitesimally close to." Therefore, the theorem could not have been stated in the formal language.

PROOF. $S_n \to S$. Formally stated, this means

$$(\forall \epsilon > 0)(\exists n_0 \in N)(\forall n \in N)(n > n_0 \Rightarrow |S_n - S| < \epsilon).$$

Now fix upon any standard $\epsilon > 0$. This also fixes n_0. Hence, for this *fixed* ϵ and n_0, it is true that

$$(\forall n \in N)(n > n_0 \Rightarrow |S_n - S| < \epsilon).$$

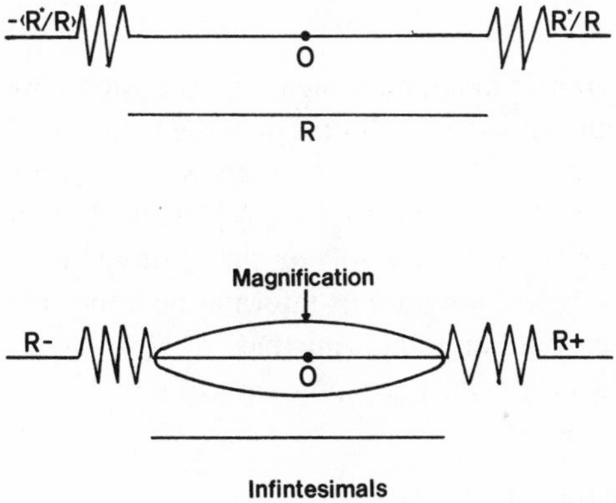

Figure 8. A heuristic view of the nonstandard number system. ΛΛΛΛ indicates fuzzy areas where we cannot precisely mark the transition between the standard and the nonstandard numbers. Such figures were first used by David Tall of the University of Warwick.

By transfer, the above is also true for $\{{}^*S_n\}$. Since any $\nu \in {}^*N - N$ satisfies $\nu > n_0$, it follows that, for any $\nu \in {}^*N - N$

$$|{}^*S_\nu - S| < \epsilon.$$

Since this is true for any standard ϵ, we must have

$${}^*S_\nu - S \simeq 0.$$

Because $\nu \in {}^*N - N$ was arbitrary, it follows that

$${}^*S_\nu - S \simeq 0 \quad \text{for all} \quad \nu \in {}^*N - N.$$

This establishes one-half of our result. Now suppose ${}^*S_\nu - S \simeq 0$ for all $\nu \in {}^*N - N$. Pick any standard $\epsilon > 0$; then we can write

$$|{}^*S_\nu - S| < \epsilon \quad \text{for all} \quad \nu \in {}^*N - N.$$

Fix $\nu_0 \in {}^*N - N$; then the following sentence is true:

$$(\exists \nu_0 \in {}^*N)(\forall n \in {}^*N)(n > \nu_0 \Rightarrow |S_\nu - S| < \epsilon).$$

By transfer, this sentence is also true in R:

$$(\exists \nu_0 \in N)(\forall n \in N)(n > \nu_0 \Rightarrow |S_\nu - S| < \epsilon).$$

But since $\epsilon > 0$ was arbitrary, the above sentence is simply the definition of convergence in R. Q.E.D.

Simple though it is, the importance of the above theorem for our purposes cannot be overstated. The first part is instructive because it tells us that nonstandard analysis preserves our intuition: If a sequence $\{S_n\}$ converges to a real number S, this means that "S_n gets arbitrarily close to S as n gets arbitrarily large." It seems only reasonable to demand that any extension of $\{S_n\}$ beyond the usual integers satisfy the corresponding statement:

> ${}^*S_n$ is infinitesimally close to S for all infinitely large n.

The second half of the theorem is much more significant. Suppose we lose the standard part of a *sequence and can observe only the behavior of the *sequence at the infinite integers, ${}^*N - N$; all we know is $\{S_\nu\}$, $\nu \in {}^*N - N$. What can we say about the original $\{S_n | n \in N\}$? It is of great importance to note that knowing the behavior only on the "purely" nonstandard integers ${}^*N - N$ nonetheless provides us information about the behavior on standard N. In the case at hand, knowing that "$S_\nu - S \simeq 0$ for all infinite $\nu \in {}^*N - N$" enabled us to deduce that, for any given real number ϵ,

$$|S_n - S| < \epsilon \text{ for all large but finite } n \in N.$$

This seemingly trivial theorem has already provided us with the key to deriving asymptotic results for large but finite economies. The method will be as follows. We begin by formulating economies ξ_ν, containing ν agents with $\nu \in {}^*N - N$. This economy contains infinitely many agents from the standard point of view but only a "finite" number of agents from the nonstandard point of view. We now prove that, for example,

> ξ_ν has an allocation infinitesimally close to a true equilibrium allocation for infinite ν.

By duplicating the reasoning of the second half of the above theorem, we can deduce that

> ξ_n, $n \in N$, has an allocation arbitrarily close to a true equilibrium, provided n is arbitrarily large.

Note that ξ_ν is an infinite nonstandard economy whereas ξ_n is a standard finite economy. Knowing the ν's has enabled us to know the n's.

The reader may well ask, "Why should we want to prove a result in the nonstandard universe in the first place?" The answer lies in recognizing that because infinite sets (in the standard sense) become *finite sets (in the nonstandard world), it is relatively simple to prove a result in the *finite world (because it behaves just like a finite world) and then transfer the result to the standard universe. As an example of such reasoning, consider the following proof of the intermediate value theorem for continuous functions. We will need to characterize continuous functions in the nonstandard framework before turning to the theorem. It is a well-known definition of continuity for real functions that

> f is continuous at x_0 if and only if
> $\{x_n\} \to x_0$ implies $\{f(x_n)\} \to f(x_0)$.

Since we have already characterized sequential continuity, we can write,

> f is continuous at x_0 if and only if
> $x \simeq x_0$ implies $f(x) \simeq f(x_0)$.

It will be a useful exercise for the reader to work out that the $\epsilon - \delta$ definition of continuity also leads to exactly the above characterization. We now turn to the

INTERMEDIATE VALUE THEOREM. *f is a continuous real-valued function defined on $[a, b]$ such that $f(a) < 0 < f(b)$. There exists c, such that $a < c < b$ and $f(c) = 0$.*

Before looking at the proof let us observe that what we wish to do is to "catch f in the act" of changing signs. An intuitive strategy is to divide $[a, b]$ into subintervals so that we can observe f more closely on each subinterval. For finite partitions of $[a, b]$, however, it is readily seen that the problem only reproduces itself and we have not advanced a whit further with this strategy. The situation is different, however, if we can take infinitely fine partitions.

PROOF. Divide $^*[a, b] = [a, b]$ into ν equal intervals, with $\nu \in {}^*N - N$, and denote the endpoints of each interval by $t_i^{(n)}$

$$t_i^{(n)} = a + n\left(\frac{b - a}{\nu}\right), \qquad n = 0, 1, 2, \ldots, \nu.$$

Note that the definition of $t_i^{(n)}$ could have been written out in the formal language and so is an internal definition.

$^*f(t_i^{(n)})$ is an internal *finite set which begins negative and ends up positive. Since internal *finite sets behave exactly like finite sets, there must be an index k at which $^*f(t_i^{(k)}) \geq 0$ for the first time. Let c denote the standard number infinitesimally close to t_i^k. Then $c \simeq t_i^k$. But $t_i^k \simeq t_i^{k-1}$, hence $t_i^{k-1} \simeq c \simeq t_i^k$.

By continuity,

$$^*f(t_i^{k-1}) \simeq {}^*f(c) \simeq {}^*f(t_i^k). \tag{1}$$

By choice of k,

$$^*f(t_i^{k-1}) < 0 \quad \text{and} \quad {}^*f(t_i^k) \geq 0. \tag{2}$$

But $^*f(c) = f(c)$ since c is standard and a standard number can be infinitesimally close to both positive and negative quantities only by being equal to zero.

More formally,

(1) implies $^\circ[^*f(t_i^{k-1})] = {}^\circ[^*f(c)] = f(c) = {}^\circ[^*f(t_i^k)]$.
(2) implies $^\circ[^*f(t_i^{k-1})] \leq 0$, $^\circ[^*f(t_i^k)] \geq 0$.

Hence $f(c) = 0$. Q.E.D.

It will be instructive for the reader to modify the above strategy to prove that every continuous function on $[a, b]$ achieves its maximum.

Robinson's Theorem

The results of the preceding section have dealt with the behavior of standard sequences when extended to the nonstandard integers. They may be said to represent a metamathematical continuity because they assert that behavior in the standard universe is not discontinuously different from behavior in the nonstandard universe. This principle is true not only for standard sequences but also for internal sequences, as indicated by the following fundamental result of Abraham Robinson. We need a preliminary definition. Let $\{X_n\}$ be a (internal or external) sequence taking values in A, that is, $X_n: {}^*N \to A$. $\bar{X} \in A$ is an F-limit of $\{X_n\}$ if, for every standard positive δ, there exists a finite natural number m such that

$$|X_n - \bar{X}| < \delta \quad \text{for} \quad n > m.$$

THEOREM (ROBINSON). *Let $\bar{X}$ be the F-limit of the internal sequence $\{X_n\}$. Then there exists an infinite natural number $\nu \in {}^*N - N$, such that $X_n \simeq \bar{X}$ for all $n \leq \nu$.*

A special case of frequent application occurs when we have an internal sequence which is infinitesimal for all $n \in N$ (0 is the F-limit). Then Robinson's theorem tells us that the sequence continues to be infinitesimal at least up to some infinite $\nu \in {}^*N - N$. For this reason, Robinson's theorem is frequently referred to as a continuation theorem or a prolongation theorem, because it tells us that we can continue or prolong an internal infinitesimal sequence beyond the standard integers.

The correct proof of Robinson's theorem provides such a robust illustration of the use of internal concepts in proving external facts that it is almost traditional to preface the correct proof by an incorrect attempt. The incorrect proof would argue as follows:

Let $A = \{n \in {}^*N | S_n \not\simeq 0\}$.
If $A = \emptyset$, any $n \in {}^*N - N$ will do as the desired ν.
If $A \neq \emptyset$, it must have a least element ν. Any $n < \nu$ will satisfy $S_n \simeq 0$. By hypothesis, ν cannot be in N, hence $(\nu - 1) \in {}^*N - N$, and $S_{\nu-1} \simeq 0$.

The difficulty with the above argument is that the set A is defined by an external concept ($\not\simeq 0$). So A need not be internal; but then A does not have to have a first element. We have to find some way to replace the set A with an internal set that will do the same job.

PROOF OF ROBINSON'S THEOREM. Let $t_n = n \cdot S_n$. t_n is internal as the product of two internal sequences. Hence $B = \{n \in {}^*N |\ |t_n| > 1\}$ is internal.

B must have a first element ν'.
$\nu' \notin N$, by the hypothesis that $S_n \simeq 0$, $\forall n \in N$.
$\therefore \nu = \nu' - 1 \in {}^*N - N$ and $t_\nu \leq 1$.
But $t_\nu \leq 1$ implies $S_\nu \leq 1/\nu \simeq 0$. Q.E.D.

The following assumption is not needed except in Chapter 10, in which the relationship between nonstandard and measure-theoretic economies is discussed, but it is convenient to state it here.

We shall assume that we are working within a comprehensive enlargement, which is a nonstandard model with the property that every function f: $*B \rightarrow R$, where $*B$ is the nonstandard extension of a set B, may be considered as the restriction to the reals of some internal nonstandard function. This may be considered as a purely auxiliary assumption. It has no substantive economic content and does not warrant extended discussion.

The property of being a comprehensive enlargement is also used to demonstrate that the nonstandard universe really is larger than the standard universe, e.g., that $R^* - R$ is not empty. The long discussion in chapter 2 motivating the construction of infinitesimals and infinitely large numbers should have prepared the reader to accept this fact.

4

Specifying the Nonstandard Economy

The commodity space most commonly used is n-dimensional Euclidean space, R^n, where n denotes the number of commodities in the model. Because commodities usually are thought of as nonnegative entities, analysis is further restricted to R^n_+, the nonnegative orthant of Euclidean n-space. Elements of this space are vectors of numbers, for example, $x = (x_1, \ldots, x_n)$. We shall denote such vectors by x, y, z, and so on. The context will suffice to distinguish scalars from vectors. Given two real numbers x, y, the meaning of the usual symbols $x > y$, $x = y$, $x \geq y$, is clear. For two vectors $x, y \in R^n$ one has to be more explicit. We shall use the convention that, for $x = (x_1, \ldots, x_n)$ and $y = (y_1, \ldots, y_n)$

$x = y$ means $x_i = y_i$ for all $i = 1, \ldots, n$.
$x \geq y$ means $x_i \geq y_i$ for all $i = 1, \ldots, n$.
$x > y$ means $x_i \geq y_i$ for all $i = 1, \ldots, n$ and for at least one j, $x_j > y_j$.
$x \gg y$ means $x_i > y_i$ for all $i = 1, \ldots, n$.

We shall be working in $^*R^n$, the nonstandard extension of R^n, and its nonnegative orthant $^*R^n_+$. By transfer, the meaning of $x > y$, $x = y$, $x \geq y$, for any two real numbers, x, y will be well defined. So too will the meaning of $x > y$, $x \gg y$, and so on, when x and y are vectors. To make effective use of nonstandard analysis, however, we shall also need some finer distinctions. For two real numbers, x, y,

$x \simeq y$ means x is infinitesimally close to y, that is, $x - y \simeq 0$.
$x \gtrsim y$ means x is either greater than y or smaller than it by an infinitesimal.
$x \gtrapprox y$ means x is greater than y by a noninfinitesimal amount.

For two vectors, x, y in R^n, we define

$x \simeq y$ means $x_i \simeq y_i$ for all $i = 1, \ldots, n$.
$x \gtrsim y$ means $x_i \gtrsim y_i$ for all $i = 1, \ldots, n$.
$x \underset{\not\simeq}{>} y$ means $x_i \geqslant y_i$ for all $i = 1, \ldots, n$ and for at least one j, $x_j \underset{\not\simeq}{>} y_j$.
$x \underset{\not\simeq}{\gg} y$ means $x_i \underset{\not\simeq}{>} y_i$ for all $i = 1, \ldots, n$.

It is important to note that any concept defined with the use of infinitesimals, such as $\simeq$, or $\gtrsim$, is an external notion. Without the use of such external concepts it would be impossible to express such intuitively obvious notions as "If a sequence $\{s_n\}$ converges to s then the terms of $\{s_n\}$ must eventually become infinitely close to s." It is the ability of nonstandard analysis to provide precise proofs of such intuitive statements that makes it a valuable analytical tool.

An *exchange economy* is fully specified when we know the number of agents in that economy as well as their initial endowments and preferences. This is the familiar textbook definition. It is one of the virtues of nonstandard analysis that exactly the same definition can be used to define a nonstandard exchange economy provided we ensure that the assignment of endowments and preferences is given in internal fashion. To prove any interesting results about such economies, however, we will have to use external concepts in defining our equilibrium notions. (If we use only internal notions, then we shall be unable to distinguish our infinite nonstandard economies from small finite economies!) Just as we saw earlier in the case of numbers and vectors, if we rest with the formal identity of standard and internal definitions we shall gain nothing by the use of nonstandard analysis. The goal of our attack is to gain external information by using internal notions as far as possible. The following discussion is meant to make the reader aware of some of the niceties involved in defining nonstandard economies. For convenience in reading, *the detailed specification of the relevant economy will be repeated in each chapter*. Let us look first at the specification of endowments.

An *initial endowment* is a vector of goods in n-space to be denoted by $I(t)$ for trader t. As such, it is open to all the qualifications about $\gtrsim$, $\gg$, and so forth noted earlier. When we speak of the entire economy, however, there is an important additional point to consider. How do we treat the aggregate resources available to the economy? If we take the view that each individual must possess a standardly finite bundle, then the aggregate of such bundles over an infinite number of individuals implies that the entire economy has an infinite initial endowment. One's first reaction may then be to say that infinite endowments violate the condition of scarcity and we have no economic problem to consider. For example, if there are ω agents,

$\omega \in {}^*N - N$, and each agent has one apple, then the entire economy has ω apples. Even though ω is an infinitely large integer in the standard sense ($\omega > n$ for all $n \in N$), in the nonstandard framework it is a finite (*finite) integer. Hence, relative to the ω nonstandard agents, scarcity does exist. Once we remember the context, the seeming paradox disappears.

It is also possible to take a different approach and insist that the aggregate resources available to society must be finite in the usual sense. But because we have an infinite number of individuals in a nonstandard economy, this will imply that most individuals can have only infinitesimal endowments.[1] If we take this approach, several theorems, such as those asserting the existence of approximate competitive equilibria, become uninteresting. After all, the infinitesimal initial endowment forces the agent to have infinitesimal wealth, and this is a considerable obstruction to one's freedom to use the market. Not only are results about such oceans of paupers uninformative, but there is a more fundamental objection to this way of modeling infinite economies. It is an axiom in the neoclassical world view that individuals are of primary importance and the correct modeling of individuals is a *sine qua non* for an acceptable model. From such a viewpoint it is definitely preferable to permit all individuals to own one apple and face the consequences than to insist that society can have only one apple and let the individuals adapt to this fact.

A *preference relation* is a complete account of the relative valuation of all possible bundles by an agent. Given any two bundles $x, y \in R^N_+$ an agent is to tell us whether x is as good as y, denoted $x \succsim y$, or y is as good as x, denoted $y \succsim x$, or both, in which case x and y are said to be indifferent, denoted $x \sim y$. This information is concisely provided if we associate with each bundle x the collection of all bundles y which are as good as x. $\succsim$ can be formally defined as

$$\succsim \; = \{(x, y) \mid y \succsim x\}.$$

When defined in this way, the preference relation is seen to be a subset of the Cartesian product of R^n_+ with itself, that is, of $\mathcal{P}(R^n_+) \times \mathcal{P}(R^n_+)$, where $\mathcal{P}(S)$ indicates the power set of the set S. $\succsim_t$ will henceforth denote the preferences of trader t; however, if the context does not require it, the subscript t will be suppressed.

If we simply transfer the above, standard, definition to the nonstandard world we obtain internal preference relations which are formally

1. This appears to be the view of Lester Telser: "Since Aumann assumes a continuum of traders, so that there are as many traders as there are real numbers and assumes a finite number of goods with a finite amount of each good, almost all of his traders have virtually no wealth" (*Competition, Collusion and Game Theory* [Chicago: Aldine, 1972], 58).

analogous to preference relations as defined in the textbooks. On some occasions, however, such transfer introduces distinctions that are too fine for our purposes. Consider, for example, the family of homothetic, internal preferences consisting of parallel straight lines with slope δ, where δ is an infinitesimal.* If we have only two goods, x_1 and x_2, then one unit of x_1 is equivalent, in utility, to δ units of x_2. With such preferences, two bundles an infinitesimal distance apart can be arbitrarily far apart in terms of utility. If, for some reason, we know that individuals are capable only of perceiving satisfactions in the domain of the real numbers, such preferences appear to be making needlessly fine distinctions. In some cases, we will therefore speak of one bundle being *monadically preferred* to another, denoted $x \}\} y$. When $x \}\} y$ is true, not only is x preferred to y but every point infinitesimally close to x is preferred to every point infinitesimally close to y, that is, $x \}\} y$ if and only if

$$(\forall u \simeq 0)(\forall v \simeq 0),\ (x + u) \} (y + v).$$

Although there are other preferences that seem to provide distinctions too fine for those who are not possessed of a nonstandard microscope, the homothetic preferences defined above also illustrate a further point. If we restrict our attention to individuals who can consume bundles only in standard Euclidean space, then any nonzero amount of x_2 alone is preferable to any finite amount of x_1. But this is precisely the condition defining lexicographic preferences. In other words, if we use our concepts with some care (especially remembering movements between internal and external), we can find a continuous utility function to represent lexicographic preferences:

$$u(x_1, x_2) = \delta x_1 + x_2,\ \delta \simeq 0.$$

It cannot be repeated too often that the skillful use of internal concepts to develop external ideas lies at the heart of useful nonstandard economic analysis.

The following description of preferences in nonstandard economies is somewhat technical and may be omitted at a first reading. (It can be omitted altogether for readers uninterested in the relationship of nonstandard and measure-theoretic economies.)

The preferences of agents will be chosen from the nonstandard extension of the space of standard preference relations on R^n_+. A preference relation, $\}$, on R^n_+ is an open subset of $R^n_+ \times R^n_+$, which is an irreflexive binary relation on R^n_+. The set of all standard preference relations is denoted by P and the nonstandard extension by $^*P$. $\not\}$ will denote the complement of $\}$ in $R^n_+ \times R^n_+$. Let $\{\not\}_n\}$ be a sequence of preferences. Then, $L_i(\not\}_n)$ and $L_s(\not\}_n)$ are defined as follows:

1. $x \in L_i(\mathfrak{z}_n)$ if and only if for each open neighborhood U of x, $U \cap \mathfrak{z}_n \neq \phi$ for all but finitely many natural members n.
2. $x \in L_s(\mathfrak{z}_n)$ if and only if for each open neighborhood U of x, $U \cap \mathfrak{z}_n = \phi$ for infinitely many natural members n.

If $L_i(\mathfrak{z}_n) = L_s(\mathfrak{z}_n) = \mathfrak{z}$, then we say that $\mathfrak{z} = \lim \mathfrak{z}_n$. This notion of convergence is topological, and the resulting topology, τ_c, on P is called the topology of closed convergence. Hildenbrand (1972) has shown that this topology is compact, metrizable, and separable; Grodal (1974) has further characterized this topology more exactly.

5 Some Preliminary Results

In trying to prove results about nonstandard economies the situation we shall most frequently encounter is the following: Each member of the set of agents, T, has a set $G(t)$ associated with itself. In the case of Pareto-optimality, for example, we consider $G(t)$ to the collection of all points preferred to a Pareto-optimal allocation. The principal result we wish to prove will involve not the individual $G(t)$ but their aggregate sum,

$$G' = \sum_{t=1}^{\omega} G(t).$$

In the Pareto-optimality problem we would like G' to be convex. This aggregate G' is not usually as well-behaved as we would like it to be, but it turns out that the average $G = 1/\omega \, \Sigma G(t)$ is generally quite well-behaved. Such average sums are the nonstandard analogues of integrals. Their importance for our results behooves a preliminary examination of some of their most important properties.

In stating and proving results about the most frequently used concepts, we shall distinguish between Q-notions and S-notions. This is simply new terminology for concepts we have previously met. Transferred internal notions are Q-notions whereas nonstandard concepts defined so as to elucidate standard ideas are S-notions. For example, given two nonstandard real numbers, x and y, if we say $x > y$ we are simply transferring the standard symbol $>$ and using a Q-notion. In this case we are not concerned whether x exceeds y by an infinitesimal or not. If, however, we say, $x \underset{\not\approx}{>} y$, we are asserting that x exceeds y by more than an infinitesimal. In this case the distance between x and y will be visible in the standard world, so such a notion can be used to distinguish standard numbers and is called an S-notion. The careful reader may have noted that the prefixes Q and * serve the same function. They both indicate transferred, internal concepts. Why this double notation should have originated is not clear, but the reader should bear it in mind.

After these preliminaries, we turn to defining infinite sums of correspondences, which we shall also call integrals. Consider a correspondence $G: T \to P(^*R^n)$. The *integral* of this correspondence will be denoted by

$$y \equiv \frac{1}{\omega} \sum_{t \in T} G(t),$$

and it will be defined to be equal to

$$\left\{ x \in {}^*R^n \,\middle|\, x = \frac{1}{\omega} \sum_{t \in T} g(t) \text{ for all } g \text{ in } F_G \right\}$$

where F_G is the set of all internal selections from

$$\prod_{t \in T} G(t),$$

the internal Cartesian product of the $G(t)$. The correspondence G is said to be *internal* if the graph of G, $\{(t, x) | t \in T, x \in G(t)\}$, is internal. G is said to be *internally bounded* if there exists an internal function g such that for all x in $G(t)$, $\|x\| \leq g(t)$ and $g(t)/\omega \simeq 0$ for all t in T.

LEMMA 1. *If $G(t)$ is internal and nonempty for all t in T, $y \neq \phi$.*

PROOF. If all the $G(t)$'s are nonempty, then y is surely nonempty for finite sums. By transfer, y is also nonempty for internal, * finite sums.

The property of nonstandard integrals that will be of most interest to us is their convexity. A set B in $^*R^n$ is said to be *Q-convex* if, for all x, y in B and all $\lambda \in {}^*(0, 1)$, there exists $z \in B$ such that $z = \lambda x + (1 - \lambda)y$. B is said to be *S-convex* if for all x, y in B, and all $\lambda \in (0, 1)$, there exists $z \in b$, such that $z \simeq \lambda x + (1 - \lambda)y$. The *Q-convex hull of B*, Q-con (B), is the set of all internal *finite convex combinations of points in B.

The following theorem will be of fundamental importance to us:

THEOREM 1 (BROWN). *If G is internally bounded, then the integral of G, $1/\omega \sum_{t \in T} G(t)$, is S-convex.*

Theorem 1 will be recognized as the nonstandard analogue of Richter's theorem on the convexity of integrals. Just as Richter's theorem is built upon Lyapunov's famous theorem on the convexity of the range of a nonatomic measure, so too is the proof of Theorem 1 built upon a nonstandard analogue of Lyapunov's theorem, due to Peter Loeb.

THEOREM 2 (LOEB). *Let T be a *finite set and for each $t \in T$, let $v(t)$ be a vector in n-space $^*R^n$ with $nv(t) \simeq 0$. For each internal $B \subseteq T$, set*

$S(B) = \Sigma_{t \in B} \nu(t)$. Then the following is true: given internal sets $B \subseteq T$ and $C \subseteq T$ and given $\lambda \in {}^*R$, $0 < \lambda < 1$, there is an internal set $D \subset T$ with $S(D) \simeq \lambda S(B) + (1 - \lambda)S(C)$.

A proof of Loeb's theorem is most easily obtained by means of the following fundamental result:

SHAPLEY-FOLKMAN THEOREM. *If $S_j, j = 1, \ldots, m$ is a collection of sets in n-dimensional space, $m > n$, and* con S_j *is the convex hull of S_j, then for any $x \in \Sigma_j$* con S_j, *there exists a representation of x of the following form:*

$$x = \sum_{J_1} y_j + \sum_{J_2} z_j,$$

where $y_j \in S_j$, $z_j \in$ con S_j, *$J_1 + J_2 = m$, and the number of elements in J_2 is no greater than n.*

Proofs of these results follow, in the reverse order of their presentation.

PROOF OF SHAPLEY-FOLKMAN THEOREM.

$$\text{Let } x = \sum_{j=1}^{m} z_j, \text{ where } z_j \in \text{con } S_j$$

$$= \sum_{j=1}^{m} \sum_{i \leq I_j} p_{ji} y_{ji}, \text{ where } y_{ji} \in S_j,\ p_{ji} \geq 0,\ \Sigma\, p_{ji} = 1. \quad (1)$$

Let I_j be the number of elements in the representation of x from S_j. Of all the representations of x of the form above choose that for which $\Sigma\, I_j$ is minimal. Suppose

$$\Sigma\, I_j > m + n \text{ i.e. } \Sigma\,(I_j - 1) > m. \quad (2)$$

Then the vectors $(b_{ji} - b_{j1})$, $1 \leq j \leq I_j$, are linearly dependent: for some real numbers r_{ji}, not all zero,

$$\sum_j \sum_{i>1} r_{ji}(y_{ji} - y_{j1}) = 0. \quad (3)$$

On multiplying (3) by a real number s and adding to (1) we get,

$$x = \sum_j \sum_i p'_{ji} y_{ji} \quad (4)$$

$$\text{where } p'_{ji} = p_{ji} + s r_{ji} \qquad i > 1$$

$$p'_{j1} = p_{j1} - s \sum_{i>1} r_{ji}.$$

By suitable choice of s, ensure that $p'_{ji} \geq 0$ for all j, i, and that at least one $p'_{ji} = 0$. But (4) is now another representation of x for which $\Sigma\, I_j$ is now smaller than for (1). This contradicts the minimality of ΣI_j in (1). Hence $\Sigma I_j \le m + n$, from whence it follows that $I_j \ne 1$ for at most n values.

Q.E.D.

PROOF OF LOEB'S THEOREM. Let the sets A_i in the Shapley-Folkman theorem be $A_i = \{v_i, 0\}$. Then $coA_i = \lambda v_i$, $0 \le \lambda \le 1$. Without loss of generality, normalize the v_i so that $\Sigma v_i = e$, where $e = (1, \ldots, 1)$. Then for any $0 \le \lambda \le 1$, $\lambda e = \Sigma \lambda v_i$, which by the Shapley-Folkman theorem equals

$$\Sigma v_i + \sum_{j=1}^{n} \lambda_j v_j .$$

As

$$0 \le \lambda_j \le 1, \qquad \left\| \sum_{j=1}^{n} \lambda_j v_j \right\| \le \max_j \| v_j \| .$$

Since $\| v_j \| \simeq 0$ for all j, $\lambda e \simeq \Sigma v_i$, and Loeb's theorem follows.

Q.E.D.

PROOF OF BROWN'S THEOREM. Suppose

$$\bar{x} = \frac{1}{\omega} \sum_T f(t) \quad \text{and} \quad \bar{y} = \frac{1}{\omega} \sum_T g(t).$$

These functions define an infinitesimal vector measure v as follows. Let

$$\tilde{x} = \frac{1}{\omega} f, \qquad \tilde{y} = \frac{1}{\omega} g.$$

Then $\bar{\mu} = (\tilde{x}, \tilde{y})$ is an infinitesimal vector measure on the set of all internal subsets of T with $\bar{\mu}(\emptyset) = (0, 0)$, $\bar{\mu}(T) = (x, y)$. By Theorem 2 (Loeb) it follows that, for any $0 < \lambda < 1$, $\exists$ internal $S \subseteq T$ such that $\bar{\mu}(S) \simeq \lambda \bar{\mu}(T) = (\lambda x, \lambda y)$ and $\bar{\mu}(T/S) \simeq (1 - \lambda)\bar{\mu}(T) = ((1 - \lambda)x, (1 - \lambda)y)$. Define,

$$\mu = \begin{cases} \tilde{x} & \text{for} \quad t \in S \\ \tilde{y} & \text{for} \quad t \in T/S \end{cases}$$

Then $\mu(T) = \tilde{x}(S) + \tilde{y}(T/S) \simeq \lambda x + (1 - \lambda)y$. But

$$\mu = \frac{h}{\omega}$$

where

$$h = \begin{cases} f & \text{for} \quad t \in S \\ g & \text{for} \quad t \in T/S \end{cases}$$

Hence,

$$\lambda x + (1 - \lambda)y \simeq \frac{1}{\omega} \sum_T h(t), \qquad \text{where} \quad h \in F_G. \qquad \text{Q.E.D.}$$

The following theorem, which relates S-convex sets to their Q-convex hulls, is also of considerable importance.

THEOREM 3. *Let $B \subseteq {}^*R^n$ be an internal, S-convex set. For any $y \in Q\text{-con}(B)$, there exists $z \in B$ such that $z \simeq y$.*

PROOF. If B is S-convex, for any $x_i \in B$ and $\lambda_i \geq 0$, $\Sigma_{i=1}^{m+1} \lambda_i = 1$, there exists $z \in B$ such that

$$z \simeq \sum_{i=1}^{m+1} \lambda_i x_i.$$

We can prove this by induction. By the definition of S-convexity the statement is true for $m + 1 = 2$. Let it hold for $m = \nu - 1$. We may suppose that $0 < \lambda_\nu < 1$; otherwise there is nothing to prove. Let

$$x' = \left(\sum_{i=1}^{\nu-1} \lambda_i x_i\right) \Big/ 1 - \lambda_\nu.$$

Since

$$\sum_{i=1}^{\nu-1} (\lambda_i / 1 - \lambda_\nu) = 1,$$

there exists r in B such that $r \simeq x'$. However,

$$\lambda_\nu x_\nu + (1 - \lambda_\nu)x' = \sum_{i=1}^{\nu} \lambda_i x_i \simeq \lambda_\nu x_\nu + (1 - \lambda_\nu)r.$$

Thus by the definition of S-convexity there exists $z \in B$ such that

$$z \simeq [\lambda_\nu x_\nu + (1 - \lambda_\nu)r] \simeq \sum_{i=1}^{\nu} \lambda_i x_i.$$

Now, by Caratheodory's theorem, any $y \in Q\text{-con}(B)$ can be written as

$$\sum_{i=1}^{n+1} \lambda_i x_i, \qquad \sum_{i=1}^{n+1} \lambda_i = 1, \qquad x_i \in B.$$

From the above there exists $z \in B$ such that

$$z \simeq \sum_{i=1}^{n+1} \lambda_i x_i = y. \qquad \text{Q.E.D.}$$

If economists can obtain convex sets, their first instinct is to find a separating hyperplane for this set. For this purpose we gather together the following theorems.

Q-SEPARATION THEOREM. *Let A, B be internal Q-convex sets in $^*R^n$ such that $A \cap B = \phi$. Then there exists $p \in {}^*R^n$, $p \neq 0$, such that $p \cdot x \geq p \cdot y$, $(\forall x \in A)(\forall y \in B)$.*

As with any theorem involving only Q-notions, the proof is of course obtained by transfer of the familiar (standard) separating, hyperplane theorem.

PROOF. See Nikaido (1968).

If $A \subseteq {}^*R^n$ is a nonstandard set such that there exists a standard point infinitesimally close to any point of A, then A is said to be *near-standard*. The S-closure of a near-standard set A is denoted $\bar{A}$. If $S(x, \delta)$ denotes the closed S-ball centered on x with radius δ and $B = S(0, 1)$, then $\bar{A}$ can be expressed as $\bar{A} = \cap\{A + \delta B \mid \delta \gtrsim 0\}$.

S-SEPARATION THEOREM. *If A is a near-standard S-convex set in $^*R^n$ and $0 \notin S\text{-int}(A)$, then there exists a standard $p \neq 0$ such that, for all $y \in A$, $p \cdot y \gtrsim 0$.*

PROOF. (i) If A is S-convex, then $\bar{A}$ is also S-convex. Suppose not; that is, there exist $x, y \in \bar{A}$ such that $z \equiv \lambda x + (1 - \lambda)y$ is not an element of A for all $\lambda \in (0, 1)$. Thus there exist $a, b \in A$ and $\delta_1 \gtrsim 0$; $\delta_2 \gtrsim 0$ such that $x = a + \delta_1 r; y = b + \delta_2 r[r \in S(0, 1)]$. Thus $\lambda x + (1 - \lambda)y = \lambda a + (1 - \lambda)b + (\lambda\delta_1 + (1 - \lambda)\delta_2)r$. But there exists $c \in A$ such that $c \simeq \lambda a + (1 - \lambda)b$. Thus certainly $c + [\lambda\delta_1 + (1 - \lambda)\delta_2]r \in \bar{A}$ for small enough δ_1, δ_2, a contradiction.

(ii) $0 \notin \text{int}(°\bar{A})$. Suppose not; that is, there exists a δ-neighborhood centered on 0 which is contained in $°\bar{A}$. Therefore the nonstandard extension of this neighborhood, the S-ball $S(0, \delta)$, is contained in the nonstandard extension of $°\bar{A}$. Thus $0 \in S\text{-int}(A)$, a contradiction. Note that $°\bar{A}$ denotes the standard part of $\bar{A}$. The reader is asked to show that

(iii) If A is an S-convex set in $^*R^n$, $°\bar{A}$ is a convex set in R^n.

We can now prove the lemma. By (i) and (iii), $°\bar{A}$ is S-convex. By (ii) $0 \notin \text{int}(°\bar{A})$. Therefore there exists a $p \in R^n$, $p \neq 0$ such that for all $x \in °\bar{A}$, $p \cdot x \geq 0$. Every $y \in \bar{A}$ can be expressed as $y = x + h$ where $x \in °\bar{A}$ and $h \simeq 0$. Thus for all $y \in \bar{A}$, we have $p \cdot y = p \cdot x + p \cdot h \geq 0 + p \cdot h \simeq 0 + ph \simeq 0$. Thus for all $y \in A$, $p \cdot y \gtrsim 0$. Q.E.D.

In proving the existence of a competitive equilibrium, the set $G(t)$ that we will associate with each agent will be t^{th} agent's demand correspondence, that is, those bundles that maximize t's happiness, given his endowments and market prices. The aspect of such correspondences that will interest us most is their upper semicontinuity, which will be defined as follows for the correspondences we deal with: A compact correspondence G of the metric space S into the metric space T is *upper semicontinuous* at x if and only if $G(x) \neq \phi$ and for every sequence $\{x_n\}$ converging to x and every sequence $\{y_n\}$ with $y_n \in G(x_n)$, there is a converging subsequence of $\{y_n\}$ whose limit belongs to $G(x)$. A correspondence is *upper semicontinuous* if it is upper semicontinuous at each point in its domain.

The fact that correspondences reflecting maximizing actions are well-behaved depends in great part on the following theorem.

THEOREM 4. *Let S, T be subsets of R^n. Let ψ be a correspondence of S into T and let $\succ_x$, $x \in S$, be an irreflexive and transitive binary relation on $\psi(x)$ with the following continuity property: The set*

$$\{(x, y, z) \in S \times T \times T \mid y, z \in \psi(x) \text{ and } y \not\succ_x z\}$$

is closed in $S \times T \times T$ ($\not\succ_x$ denotes the complement of $\succ_x$).

If the set $\psi(x)$ is compact, then the set $\beta(x)$ of maximal elements for $\succ_x$ in $\psi(x)$ is nonempty and compact and the correspondence β is upper-semicontinuous at every point x where ψ is continuous.

PROOF. See Berge (1966).

The following special case of the above theorem, where $\succ_x$ is a continuous function, is well known and is important enough to be stated separately as a theorem.

THEOREM 5. *Let the correspondence of ψ of S into T be compact-valued and continuous and let $f: S \times T \to R$ be a continuous real function. Then*

(a) *The function $x :\to m(x) = \max\{f(x, y) \mid y \in \psi(x)\}$ is continuous.*

(b) *The correspondence $x :\to \{y \in \psi(x, y) = m(x)\}$ is nonempty, compact-valued, and upper-semicontinuous.*

Since we will need to aggregate the behavior of individuals, the following result is also necessary.

THEOREM 6. *If $G = \Sigma G_i$, $i = 1, \ldots, n$, where each G_i is an upper-semicontinuous correspondence with the same domain, then G is also an upper-semicontinuous correspondence.*

PROOF. See Nikaido (1968).

Finally, since we cannot prove that *every* agent is very close to equilibrium, we will need to neglect a small proportion of the individuals in an infinite economy. Theorem 7 tells us that neglecting such small proportions will influence our economy in infinitesimal fashion. We need some preliminary definitions. Let $T = \{1, \ldots, \omega\}$ denote an initial segment of the nonstandard integers. I is an internal function from T to $^*R^n_+$ with the following properties:

$$\text{(i)}\quad \frac{1}{\omega}\sum_T I(t) \gg\!\!\!\!\not\; 0$$

$$\text{(ii)}\quad (\forall S \subseteq T)\left(\frac{|S|}{\omega} \simeq 0 \Rightarrow \frac{1}{\omega}\sum_{t\in S} I(t) \simeq 0\right)$$

If $I(t)$ is interpreted as the initial endowment of agent t, then (i) says that there exists a nonnegligible amount of each commodity in the economy, and (ii) says that negligible subsets of traders own negligible proportions of the total endowment. Finally, let x denote an internal function from T to $^*R^n_+$ such that

$$\frac{1}{\omega}\sum x(t) = \frac{1}{\omega}\sum I(t).$$

x will later be called an allocation and $x(t)$ denotes the commodity bundle assigned to trader t.

THEOREM 7 (ANDERSON). (i) *For any allocation* x, *there exists* $M \in N$ *such that*

$$\frac{1}{\omega}\sum x(t) \le Me$$

(ii) *the set*

$$V' = \left\{t \in T \,\middle|\, \frac{X(t)}{\omega} \simeq 0\right\}$$

is contained in an internal set V *with*

$$\frac{|V|}{\omega} \simeq 0.$$

PROOF. (i) Let

$$\theta = \left\{n \in {}^*N \,|\, S \subset T, \frac{|S|}{\omega} < \frac{1}{n}, \frac{1}{\omega}\sum_S I(t) \le e\right\}.$$

θ is internal and contains $^*N - N$. Its first element, k, must be in N. Partition T into $(k + 1)$ internal subsets A_i all of size less than $1/k$. Then

$$\frac{1}{\omega}\sum_T I(t) = \frac{1}{\omega}\sum_{i=0}^{k}\sum_{t\in A_i} I(t) \le (k + 1)e.$$

Set $M = k + 1$ to complete the proof of (i).

(ii) Suppose $\nu \in {}^*N - N$ with $\nu/\omega \simeq 0$. Define $V = \{t \in T \mid X(t) > \nu e\}$. V is internal and contains V'. If

$$\frac{|V|}{\omega} \not\simeq 0$$

then

$$\frac{1}{\omega} \sum_T X(t) \geq \frac{|V|}{\omega}. \qquad \text{Or,}$$

$\eta e > Me$, which contradicts (i). Q.E.D.

II

FARRELL'S CONJECTURES

Chapters 6 and 7 are taken up with Farrell's conjectures on Pareto-optimality and existence without convexity assumptions on preferences. Chapter 6, on Pareto-optimality, is the easiest chapter in this monograph. I have presented just one result in its most basic setting in order to illustrate clearly how closely nonstandard arguments follow the usual proof of the second basic theorèm of Welfare Economics. Chapter 6 concludes by showing how asymptotic results may be derived from results for a nonstandard economy.

Chapter 7, by contrast, is a relatively hard chapter, and the reader is assumed to have some familiarity with the technical issues involved in proofs of the existence of a competitive equilibrium. An extensive discussion of the manner in which nonstandard analysis succeeds in providing a simple and direct proof precedes the actual proof. This is followed by some subsidiary results for which the argument, though rigorous, is not written up with complete formality. If the reader finds the argument plausible, there will be no difficulty in translating the argument into symbols. The second part of this chapter introduces a productive economy and shows how to extend the earlier argument in this context. For the sake of simplicity, this is the only discussion in the monograph of the problems of production.

6

Pareto-Optimality in Large Markets

One of the fundamental theorems of Welfare Economics states that if tastes and technology are convex and markets are universal, any Pareto-efficient allocation can be achieved as a competitive equilibrium by a suitable reallocation of initial resources. Farrell conjectured that this proposition remains approximately true if convexity is replaced by the weakened convexity assumption that "there are no indivisibilities large relative to the economy"; thus Farrell claimed that he had "broadened the basis of the theory in that it is now valid if either the convexity assumption or the multiplicity assumption holds" (1959:390). In this chapter I provide a set of conditions under which Farrell's conjecture can be proved.

Large but Finite Exchange Economies

A finite exchange economy, ξ_k, consists of a set of k traders, $\{T_k\}$, where k is a finite natural number, whose initial endowments and preferences are restricted to the commodity space R^n_+, n being a finite natural number. The endowment of the tth trader will be denoted by $I(t)$ and his preference relation by $\succsim_t$. Our objective is to formalize notions of approximate Pareto-optimality for ξ_k and to see if these approximate Pareto optima can be achieved by the price system as the number of traders, k, tends to infinity.

Under the classical definition, an allocation X is said to be Pareto-optimal if there does not exist any other allocation Y that makes at least one trader better off without making any trader worse off. Thus our search for approximate notions has to revolve around a formalization of one or all of the following factors:

(a) an allocation,
(b) a trader being made better off,
(c) a measure of the set of traders, B, being made better off, and
(d) a measure of the set of traders, C, being made worse off.

We can easily see that under the classical definition the above are made precise respectively as

(a) $\sum_{t \in T_k} X(t) = \sum_{t \in T_k} I(t)$,
(b) $Y(t) \succ_t X(t)$,
(c) $|B| \geq 1$, where $|B|$ denotes the number of traders in B, and
(d) $|C| = 0$.

In the chapter on Edgeworth's conjecture we shall try to find approximate results for various versions of each of (a), (b), (c), and (d). In this chapter we stick to the simplest and most basic result.

A nonstandard exchange economy, ξ_ω, consists of a pair of functions I and $\succsim$ satisfying A(i) to A(iii) below, where

$$I: T \to {}^*R^n_+ \text{ and } \succsim: T \to \mathcal{P}({}^*R^n_+ \times {}^*R^n_+)$$

and $\mathcal{P}({}^*R^n_+)$ denotes the power set of ${}^*R^n_+$.

A(i) to A(iii) are as follows:

A(i) the function indexing the initial endowments, $I(t)$, is internal.
A(ii) $(1/\omega) \sum_{t \in T} I(t) \not\gg 0$.
A(iii) The relation

$$Q = \{(t, \succsim_t) | t \in T, \succsim \in {}^*R^n_+ \times {}^*R^n_+\}$$

is internal. Furthermore, $\succsim_t$ satisfies iii.1 and iii.2 below.

iii.1. $\succsim_t$ is reflexive for all t in T and there exists τ in T such that $X(\tau)$ is a nonsatiation consumption for τ.

iii.2. For all t in T, $\succsim_t$ is reflexive and monotonic, that is, $x \gg y$ implies $x \succ_t y$.

An allocation Y is an internal function from T into ${}^*R^n_+$ such that

$$\sum_{t \in T} Y(t) \leq \sum_{t \in T} I(t).$$

In what follows I shall speak of a property being true for almost all t in T. By this I mean that the property is true for an internal set of traders $K \subseteq T$ such that $|K|/\omega \asymp 1$.

We can now state our result.[1]

1. Weaker versions of the above theorem were presented in Khan and Rashid (1975); the earlier results have been strengthened along the lines suggested by Khan and Rashid (1978).

THEOREM 1. *If* ξ_ω *satisfies Assumption* iii.1, *then corresponding to any Pareto-optimal allocation X of* ξ_ω, *there exists a standard vector* $p \neq 0$ *such that for almost all t in T,*

$$p \cdot x(t) \gtrsim p \cdot X(t) \qquad \forall x(t) \succsim_t X(t).$$

COROLLARY 1. *If* ξ_ω *satisfies Assumption* iii.2 *instead of* iii.1, *then* $p > 0$.

To picture the import of these results let us recall that a commodity bundle is efficient at a set of prices p if any other commodity bundle preferred to it costs more. Thus in figure 9, $X(t)$ is efficient. If X is an allocation such that $X(t)$ is efficient for almost all t in T, then X is said to be an efficiency equilibrium. We will say that a commodity bundle is ϵ-efficient if all preferred commodity bundles cost more or do not cost very much less than it. In figure 9, X_ϵ is ϵ-efficient. If X_ϵ is an allocation such that $X_\epsilon(t)$ is ϵ-efficient for almost all t in T, then X_ϵ is said to be an ϵ-efficiency equilibrium. We know that in general we cannot sustain a Pareto-optimal allocation of a finite nonconvex economy as an efficiency equilibrium. Theorem 1 says that the Pareto-optimal allocations of such an economy can be sustained as an approximate efficiency equilibrium or an ϵ-efficiency equilibrium. Further, the larger the economy, the finer the approximation. Note that we only assume that the preferences are reflexive and that the Pareto-optimal allocation is not a bliss point for at least one trader.

A little care is needed when interpreting Theorem 1 in terms of price decentralization of a Pareto-optimal allocation. The problem is that at the

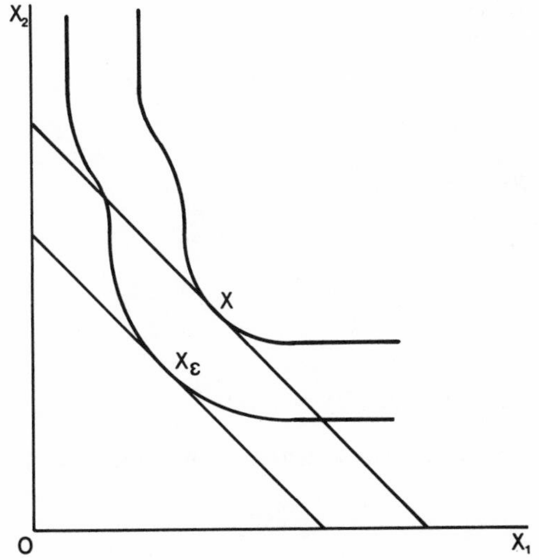

Figure 9. An optimal and an approximately optimal bundle.

prices p and a fictitious allowance to each trader of $p \cdot X(t)$ units, each agent may buy a commodity bundle very different from $X(t)$. That p can have zero coordinates makes matters worse. It should be remembered, however, that this difficulty is also present for convex markets. It is only when the preferences of each trader are strictly convex that the planner can expect each trader to pick the Pareto-optimal commodity bundles when he gives out the prices p.

An alternative interpretation can be given. Consider a situation in which every trader holds a Pareto-optimal commodity bundle. This outcome may have been achieved by some planning process that is not our concern. The question we are interested in is whether there exist some set of prices under which this outcome will be stable in the sense that none of the traders will want to get rid of their Pareto-optimal bundles. The answer of Theorem 1 is yes, provided there is also a cost to trading. This cost may be in the form of a lump-sum tax on trading, a transaction cost, or whatever. Under this cost no trader, except a small deviant set, will have an incentive to sell his Pareto-optimal commodity bundle $X(t)$ and buy a different bundle.

PROOF OF THEOREM 1. Let X be a Pareto-optimal allocation.

I. The first step lies in showing that any aggregate bundle which is Pareto-preferred costs too much. Define,

$$F(t) = [x(t) \in {}^*R^n_+ \,|\, x(t) \succsim X(t)] \qquad \forall t \neq \tau.$$

$$G(t) = F(t) - X(t).$$

Note that $0 \in F(t)$ for all $t \neq \tau$.

$$F(\tau) = [x(t) \in {}^*R^n_+ \,|\, x(\tau) \succ X(\tau)]$$

$$G(\tau) = F(\tau) - X(\tau).$$

Define $G' \equiv \Sigma\, G(t)$.
Suppose $0 \in \Sigma\, G(t)$.
Then there exists $h(t) \in G(t)$ such that

$$h(t) \succsim X(t) \qquad \text{for all } t$$

$$h(\tau) \succ X(\tau)$$

and

$$\Sigma[h(t) - X(t)] = 0 \quad \text{or} \quad \Sigma\, h(t) = \Sigma\, X(t) = \Sigma\, I(t).$$

So $h(t)$ is a feasible and Pareto-superior redistribution. This contradicts the Pareto-optimality of X.

Although $\Sigma\, G(t)$ need not be convex, by Brown's Theorem

$$G = \frac{1}{\omega} \Sigma\, F(t)$$

is S-convex. Hence there exists a standard vector $p \neq 0$ such that

$$p \cdot y \gtrsim 0 \qquad \text{for all } y \in G$$

II. The second step consists in showing that Pareto-preferred bundles are too expensive for almost all individuals.

Suppose $p \cdot y(t) \lnsim 0$ for a nonnegligible set of traders S. Since $0 \in G(t)$ for all $t \neq \tau$ and $0 \in$ closure $G(\tau)$ for $t = \tau$, we can pick $y(t) = 0\ \forall t \notin S$; if $\tau \notin S$ set $y(t) = \delta \cdot e$ for τ, for δ arbitrarily small.

$p \cdot y$ reduces to

$$\frac{1}{\omega} \sum_{S} p \cdot y(t) + \delta \lnsim 0$$

since $p \cdot y(t) \lnsim 0$ for all $t \in S$ and $|S|/\omega \neq 0$.

This contradicts $p \cdot y \gtrsim 0\ \forall y \in G$.

Hence $p \cdot y(t) \gtrsim 0$ for all but a negligible set of traders, that is, $p \cdot x(t) \gtrsim p \cdot X(t)$ for almost all traders. Q.E.D.

Proof of Corollary 1. Since all conditions of the theorem apply, we must have $p \cdot y \gtrsim 0$, $\forall y \in G$.

Suppose p_1 is negative, that is, $p_1 \lnsim 0$. Set $y(t) = 0$ for all t except $t = \tau$ and pick $y(\tau) = (\omega, 1, \ldots, 1)$. Then

$$p \cdot y = \frac{1}{\omega}(p_1\omega + p_2 + \cdots + p_n)$$

$$= p_1 + \frac{(1 - p_1)}{\omega} \lnsim 0$$

thereby contradicting $p \cdot y \gtrsim 0$, $\forall y \in G$. Q.E.D.

To see the implications of Theorem 1 for finite economies, let us define a sequence of finite economies $\{\xi_k\}$, $k \in N$ (ξ_k contains k traders) such that, when $\{\xi_k\}$ is extended to the nonstandard universe, we obtain ξ_ω, which satisfy the hypotheses of Theorem 1. Let then $\{\xi_k\}$ be a sequence of finite economies such that, for each $k \in N$, the initial endowments of each agent in ξ_k lies in R^n and the preference of each agent is reflexive. For each ξ_k the aggregate initial endowment will be assumed to satisfy

$$\frac{1}{k} \Sigma\, I(t) \gnsim 0.$$

THEOREM 2. *Let* $\{\xi_k\}$ *be a sequence of finite economies defined as above. If* X_k *is a Pareto-optimal allocation in* ξ_k *such that at least one trader is not at a bliss point, then for all k larger than some* k_0, *there exists a set of prices* p_k *which approximately prices out* X_k. *That is,*

$$(\forall\epsilon > 0)(\exists k_0)(\forall k \geq k_0)(\exists p_k)(\exists S_k \subseteq T_k)\left(\frac{|S_k|}{|T_k|} \geq 1 - \epsilon\right)$$

$$((x \succsim X_k(t) \Rightarrow |p_k \cdot x - p_k \cdot X_k(t)| < \epsilon).$$

PROOF. Suppose the result is false. Then there exists $\epsilon > 0$, $\epsilon \in R$, such that

$$(\forall k \in N)(\exists p_k)(\exists S_k \subseteq T_k)\left(\frac{|S_k|}{|T_k|} \geq 1 - \epsilon\right)$$

$$\cap\ (x \succsim X_k(t) \Rightarrow |p_k \cdot x - p_k \cdot X_k(t)| < \epsilon).$$

On transferring this statement to the nonstandard universe, we get a sentence which is cumbersome to read but which says that there exists a Pareto-optimal allocation in ξ_ω which cannot be ϵ-priced out for some standard ϵ. But this contradicts Theorem 1. Q.E.D.

The above procedure is mimicked whenever we wish to obtain a result for large but finite economies from a result true for nonstandard economies. It always involves writing down an appropriate sentence $\mathcal{S}$ which states that the large, finite economies become better behaved as n increases. We then assume this statement is false in the standard world so that its negation, not-$\mathcal{S}$, is true. Not-$\mathcal{S}$ is then transferred to the nonstandard world, where it immediately contradicts the already proved result for the nonstandard economy. Since the assumption of not-$\mathcal{S}$ being true led to a contradiction, we are ready to assert that $\mathcal{S}$ is true. But $\mathcal{S}$ is exactly the asymptotic result for large, finite economies that we want. It is tedious to repeat this argument over and over, so I shall work it out only once more, for the results on the pricing out of core allocations, and leave the reader to fill out the asymptotic versions of other results proved here.

7

The Existence of Equilibrium

In the preceding chapter we examined the interrelationships between the competitive equilibria and Pareto-optimal allocations of an infinite economy, and we shall subsequently look at the relationship between core allocations and competitive equilibria. Such exercises are of very little significance if it cannot also be shown that the competitive equilibria actually exist—that we have not been theorizing about the empty set. We therefore turn in this chapter to proving the existence of competitive equilibria in infinite economies, a much harder mathematical problem. The first section treats an exchange economy; the second section extends this to the case of an economy with production.

The notion of general equilibrium familiar to all economic theorists is that of a price vector, p, and a corresponding commodity bundle, $X(t)$, for each agent such that $X(t)$ maximizes preferences within the budget set of t[1] and such that the collection of such commodity bundles satisfies the aggregate constraint $\Sigma X(t) \leq \Sigma I(t)$. That is, the sum total of all the commodities demanded by the consumers must be less than or equal to the sum total of all commodities agents possessed to start with. General equilibrium therefore necessitates fulfilling the following conditions; each stipulation that has an approximate equivalent is noted by italics: *All* agents choose a *maximal bundle* within their *budget set* and the aggregate demand is *not greater than* the aggregate supply. By varying *all* to *almost all* or by weakening *maximal* to *almost maximal* or *budget set* to *approximate budget set*

This chapter is based largely on my dissertation, Rashid (1976), and on Khan and Rashid (1982).

1. Of course, the $X(t)$ depend upon p, the price vector, but this is suppressed for simplicity of notation.

or by permitting aggregate demand to *exceed* aggregate supply by a small amount or by combining some of all the above notions, we can generate notions of approximate equilibria. It is an indication of the strength of the first theorem to be proved that we require only to relax the condition that aggregate excess demand be nonpositive in order to obtain an equilibrium. Furthermore, although the excess demand may be a large positive amount in absolute terms, it will be negligible when compared with the size of the economy.

The second theorem will then examine what we must give up if we insist on the nonpositivity of aggregate excess demand. Suppose we let the burden of this approximation fall on the requirement that *all* traders have maximal bundles. *Some* traders must now be moved away from their previous maximal bundles, and it will be picturesque to call these unfortunates "deviants." Theorem 2 will show the existence of an equilibrium in which all traders except the deviants have maximal bundles in their budget sets and aggregate excess demand is nonpositive. We will not only show that the number of deviants is negligible relative to the number of traders but will also have placed a bound on the absolute number of these deviants. The extent of deviance may, however, be large. By enlarging the class of deviants, it is possible to ensure the nonpositivity of aggregate excess demand by making the extent of deviance of each trader smaller than any preassigned real number. This would not be of much interest were it not that the total number of even this expanded class of deviants can be kept a negligible proportion of the total number of traders.

A nonstandard exchange economy ξ_ω is defined, as before, by an internal set of traders, $T = \{1, \ldots, \omega\}$ and a pair of internal functions I and $\}$ denoting the initial endowment and the preferences, respectively, of each trader. We shall make the following assumptions on $I(t)$ and $\}_t$.

(i) $\dfrac{I(t)}{\omega} \simeq 0$, for all $t \in T$.

(ii) $\dfrac{1}{\omega} \sum_T I(t) \not\simeq 0$.

(iii) For all t in T

(α) $\}_t$ is a partial order.

(β) If $x > y$, then $x \}_t y$.

(γ) $\}_t$ is Q-continuous; for all $x, y \in {}^*R^n_+$, $\{z \in {}^*R^n_+ | z \}_t y\}$ and $\{z \in {}^*R^n_+ | x \}_t z\}$ are Q-open subsets.

A *competitive equilibrium* for ξ_ω consists of a pair (p, X), where p is a vector in the unit simplex of ${}^*R^n_+$ and X is an allocation with $X(t)$ maximal in the budget set $B_p(t)$ with respect to $\succ_t$ for all traders in T—that is,

$$\frac{1}{\omega}\Sigma\, X(t) \simeq \frac{1}{\omega}\Sigma\, I(t)$$

and for all t in T, $\nexists y \in B_p(t)$ such that $y \succ_t X(t)$, where $B_p(t) = \{x \mid p \cdot x \leq p \cdot I(t)\}$.

THEOREM 1. *There exists a competitive equilibrium for* ξ_ω.

Discussion of Proof

The major mathematical tool used in proving existence is the Kakutani fixed-point theorem. This well-known theorem guarantees us the existence of a fixed point if we map a compact, convex set into itself by means of a nonempty convex-valued, upper-semicontinuous correspondence. The problem thus is to choose a suitable compact, convex set and an upper-semicontinuous correspondence whose fixed point will be a competitive equilibrium.

In economics, the compact, convex set is often the Cartesian product of price and quantity space, with excess demands being represented in quantity space. Since prices are assumed to lie in the unit simplex, the convexity and compactness of this component is trivial. Problems arise only with regard to the quantity component because (a) when a price is zero, nothing prevents an individual from purchasing an unlimited quantity of the commodity, and (b) if the initial endorsements can grow without bound, as they can if initial endowments are integrable, then the quantities demanded can also grow without bound. For both these reasons, most existing proofs for infinite economies, whether measure-theoretic or nonstandard, consider a sequence of economies with truncated consumption sets.[2] They consider a sequence of economies $\{\xi_k\}_{k=1}^{\infty}$ with the consumption set in ξ_k being artificially bounded by a suitable k-cube. For these economies one can apply the standard tools of general equilibrium theory and obtain equilibrium price and quantity allocations, $\langle p_k, X_k\rangle$. The major difficulty lies in extracting a suitable subsequence k_j from the given sequence of $\langle p_k, X_k\rangle$ such that for large enough k_j in this subsequence $\langle p_{k_j}, X_{k_j}\rangle$ is a competitive equilibrium for the original economy.

An elegant alternative to truncating consumption sets was discovered by Werner Hildenbrand (1974). Instead of examining the behavior of maximal elements for *all* prices, he studied the behavior of maximal elements

2. Weddepohl (1977) is the only exception known to me.

when prices are restricted to lie in the interior of the price simplex. Because the mappings behave badly only when one or more prices is allowed to be zero, this restriction of the mapping to the interior of the price simplex is an elegant way of avoiding the unbounded property of the maximal elements. As far as the nonstandard proofs are concerned, the two methods, one involving truncated consumption sets and the other involving the truncated price simplex, are almost entirely equivalent. After providing a more detailed description of the truncation procedure for consumption sets, it will be possible to show why the two methods achieve the same end in different ways. The first theorem to be proved will then combine the two methods to prove a simple yet general theorem on the existence of equilibrium.

Although both measure-theoretic and nonstandard proofs employ the same truncation procedure for consumption sets, the role played by truncation is not identical in the two methods. For measure-theoretic economies, convexity of the average aggregate demand is guaranteed by the well-known Lyapunov theorem on the convexity of the range of a vector measure, and truncation serves only to provide compactness. For nonstandard economies, however, Loeb's theorem enables truncation to provide both convexity and compactness simultaneously.

LOEB'S THEOREM. *Let T be an internal star-finite set and, for each $t \in T$, let $v(t)$ be a vector in n-space $*R^n$ with $nv(t) \simeq 0$. For each internal set B T, let $S(B) = \Sigma_{t\in B}\, v(t)$. Then the following is true: Given internal sets $B \subseteq T$ and $C \subseteq T$ and given $\lambda \in *R$ with $\lambda \in (0, 1)$, there exists an internal set $D \subseteq T$ with $S(D) \simeq \lambda S(B) + (1 - \lambda)S(C)$.*

In our applications

$$v(t) = \frac{X(t)}{\omega}, \qquad X(t) \in *R^n,$$

and $v(t) \simeq 0$ is obtained by confining $X(t)$ to some k-cube, $k \in N$; however, $v(t) \simeq 0$ also when $X(t)$ is confined to an appropriate ν-cube in $*R_n$, $\nu \in *N - N$. This observation suggests that by choosing a suitable ν, we can dispense with the process of a sequence of truncations and make do instead with a single truncation—that is, we begin by showing the existence of a competitive equilibrium for an economy in which everyone is forced to choose bundles within the ν-cube and then show that if we remove this constraint, no one will have an incentive to move.

To transfer the Kakutani fixed-point theorem, we need Q-compact, Q-convex sets (where the Q-prefix indicates a notion derived by transfer of a standard notion). Any $\nu \in *N - N$ as our bound will provide us with a Q-compact set. We cannot, however, choose ν so large that Loeb's theorem does not hold or we will be unable to guarantee convexity of the aggregate demand sets. The bound ν must, however, be large enough to include not only all $I(t)$ but also all bundles $X(t)$ chosen by individuals with endowment $I(t)$. (We shall show later that at our truncated equilibrium all prices will be noninfinitesimally positive; this in turn implies that $\|X(t) - I(t)\| / \|I(t)\|$ is finite.) If we can pick a ν "infinitely" larger than $\max \|I(t)\|$ while keeping ν "small" relative to the number of traders—while preserving $\nu/\omega \simeq 0$—we shall be done.

Let

$$m = \max_{t \in T}[\sum_{j=1} I^j(t)].$$

The maximum exists and is achieved because $I(t)$ is an internal function over a *finite set of points. By assumption (i), $m/\omega \simeq 0$. We shall pick ν as the size of our bounding cube, where ν is defined by $\nu^2 = m\omega$. This implies that $(\nu/\omega)^2 = m/\omega \simeq 0$. Therefore, $\nu/\omega \simeq m/\nu \simeq 0$.

By restricting maximal bundles to lie within the cube of size ν, we ensure that no individual chooses a bundle that is large relative to ω—that is, $X(t)/\omega \not\simeq 0$. If some prices are very small, and infinitesimal, there will, however, be points that are simply disallowed, and this opens the unpleasant possibility that there may be a point in the region denoted θ that is preferred to any point in the cube (figure 10). There is no reasonable way of ruling out this outcome, so we do not permit such outcomes to occur—we limit all the prices we shall consider so that their budget sets will always be interior to the cube. In R^2 for any price, p', if the budget set for (m, m) lies

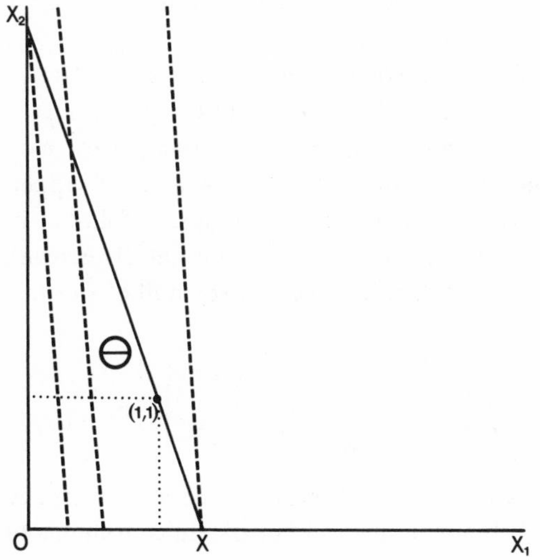

Figure 10. Infinitesimal prices that can lead to optima outside the bounding cube.

inside (ν, ν) so will the budget set for all agents lie inside (ν, ν) at prices p'. To get the smallest price that will still keep agents within the cube, we need, therefore, consider only (m, m). Consider the first coordinate; p' must satisfy $p_1'\nu < m$ or $p_1' < m/\nu \simeq 0$. In other words, so long as we restrict ourselves to prices in the interior of the simplex $S_\eta = \{p\epsilon{}^*R^2_+, \Sigma\, p_i = 1$, and $p_i \geq 1/\eta$, where $\eta = \left[\frac{\nu}{m}\right]$, the smallest integer greater than $\nu/m\}$, we can be sure that the commodity bundles chosen will be maximal bundles. Two points about this procedure should be noted: first, we consider only strictly positive price vectors; second, and more important, every truncated price simplex argument must use a cube, either implicitly or explicitly, and it therefore seems artificial to speak of either method as the more general one. (Indeed, when dealing with production we cannot avoid using an explicit cube to bound production possibilities.)

PROOFS. Define the following sets and correspondences.

$$S_\eta = \left\{p\epsilon{}^*R^n_+ \,|\, \Sigma\, p_i = 1,\, p_i \geq \frac{1}{\eta}\right\} \quad \text{and} \quad \frac{1}{\eta} = \left[\frac{m}{\nu}\right]$$

$$M = \{x\epsilon{}^*R^n_+ \,|\, x \leq \nu e,\ \nu \text{ chosen as before—}\nu^2 = m\omega\}$$

That both S and M are internal, Q-compact, and Q-convex is obvious.

$$B_p(t) = \{X\epsilon{}^*R^n_+ \,|\, p \cdot X \leq p \cdot I(t)\}$$

$$C_p(t) = B_p(t) \cap M.$$

$$D_p(t) = \{X(t)\epsilon C_p(t) \,|\, \nexists y\epsilon C_p(t) \text{ such that } y \succ X(t)\} \text{ if } p \cdot I(t) > 0$$

$$= \{C_p(t)\} \qquad \text{if } p \cdot I(t) = 0$$

Since $\succ_t$ is internal, $D_p(t)$ is a nonempty, upper-semicontinuous, internal correspondence by transfer of Theorem 5.4.

$\tilde{\psi}: S_\eta \to M$; $\tilde{\psi}(p) = \{x\epsilon{}^*R^n_+$ there exists an internal $X(t): T \to {}^*R^n_+, x = 1/\omega\, \Sigma\, X(t)$ and $X(t)\epsilon D_p(t)$ for all $t\epsilon T\}$—that is, $\tilde{\psi}(p) = 1/\omega\, \Sigma\, D_p(t)$.

$\tilde{\psi}(p)$ is the sum of a *finite set of internal correspondences, each member of which is semicontinuous. Since the sum of a set of upper-semicontinuous correspondences is upper-semicontinuous, it follows, by transfer, that $\tilde{\psi}(p)$ is upper-semicontinuous. It is also internal. By Brown's theorem $\tilde{\psi}(p)$ is S-convex. Let $\tilde{\psi}(p)$ denote the Q-convex hull of $\tilde{\psi}(p)$.

$$\phi: M \to S_\eta$$

$$\phi(x) = \left\{p\epsilon S_\eta \,|\, \forall q\epsilon S_\eta,\ p \cdot \left[x - \frac{1}{\omega}\Sigma\, I(t)\right] \geq q \cdot \left[x\, \Sigma\, \frac{1}{\omega}\, I(t)\right]\right\}.$$

$\phi(x)$ is the set of maximizers of a linear function over a Q-compact, Q-convex set. Hence $\phi(x)$ is both nonempty and upper-semicontinuous by theorem 5.5. The convexity of the set of maximizers of a linear function over a compact, convex set is a well-known result, and, by transfer, it ensures the Q-convexity of $\phi(x)$.

Define $\theta = \phi x \psi : S_\eta \times M \rightarrow S_\eta \times M$—that is, $\theta(p, x) = \phi(x) \times \psi(p)$. From what we have said above, θ is an internal Q-compact, Q-convex valued, upper-semicontinuous correspondence from an internal Q-compact, Q-convex set into itself; hence the transferred version of Kakutani's theorem applies and θ must have a fixed point. This concludes the first step of the existence proof.

Equilibria with All Agents Maximal

Let (p, x) be the fixed point of θ. Since $\tilde{\psi}(p)$ is S-convex, by Brown's theorem there exists an internal function $X(t)$ and that $x \simeq 1/\omega\, X(t)$ and $X(t) \in Dp(t)$. Because $X(t)$ is already maximal in $Dp(t)$ and $Bp(t) \subseteq Dp(t)$ by choice of S_η, we only need to show that $1/\omega\, \Sigma\, X(t) \leq 1/\omega\, \Sigma\, I(t)$ to complete the proof.

Because $p \cdot X(t) \leq p \cdot I(t)$ for all t in T, if we define $b = 1/\omega\, \Sigma\, I(t) - 1/\omega\, X(t)$, we must have $p \cdot b \geq 0$. By definition of ϕ, $(\forall q \in S_\eta)\ (p \cdot b \leq q \cdot b)$—that is, $0 < q \cdot b$.

Suppose some component of b, say $b_1 < 0$. Set $q = (1 - \frac{(n-1)}{\eta}$, $n - 1/\eta, 1/\eta, \ldots, 1/\eta)$. Then

$$q \cdot b = b_1\left(1 - \frac{n-1}{\eta}\right) + b_2 \frac{1}{\eta} + \cdots + b_n \cdot \frac{1}{\eta}$$

$$= b_1\left(1 - \frac{n-1}{\eta}\right) + \frac{1}{\eta}(b_2 + \cdots + b_n).$$

b_j, $j \geq 2$, is given by $1/\omega\, \Sigma\, I^j(t) - 1/\omega\, \Sigma\, X^j(t)$. As $X^j(t) \in R^n$, $b_j \leq 1/\omega\, \Sigma\, I^j(t) \leq C_j$ for some $C_j \in R_t$.

$$\therefore\ 1/\eta(b_2 + \cdots + b_n) \leq 1/\eta(C_2 + \cdots + C_n) \simeq 0,$$

since $C_j \in R_+$, but then $q \cdot b < 0$, contradicting $q \cdot b \geq 0$. By repeating the above for each coordinate, we get $b > 0$. This concludes the proof of Theorem 1.

REMARK 1. Even if the "equilibrium" price for a commodity should be zero, we are forcing its price to be a positive infinitesimal.

REMARK 2. Since we do not look at the maximal elements for all prices, a slight (infinitesimal) change in prices can produce a large (infinite) change in $X(t)$.

REMARK 3. In choosing a preferred point, every coalition can use any mechanism it wishes. In particular, it could use the price mechanism; since the above equilibrium does not consider all prices in the simplex, it will not provide the usual equivalence theorems between the core and competition equilibria.

The following example will help bring out some of the significant properties of the above definition of equilibrium. All traders are identical with $I(t) = (1, 1)$. Every preference consists of parallel straight lines with slope $1/\omega$.

At prices $(1 - 1/\eta, 1/\eta)$, only commodity 1 will be consumed—that is,

$$X(t) = \left(1 + \frac{\frac{1}{\eta}}{1 - \frac{1}{\eta}}, 0 \right).$$

Every consumer has positive excess demand, but since this is an infinitesimal amount, it does not matter when added up and weighted by $1/\omega$.

Equilibria with Nonpositive Aggregate Excess Demands

Define an *ε-Rothenberg equilibrium* as a triple (p, X, K) where $p \geq 0$ is a price vector, X an allocation such that $X(t)$ is maximal in $Bp(t)$ for all t in K, with $|K|/\omega \geq 1 - \epsilon$. We will now prove

THEOREM 1B. *There exists an ε-Rothenberg equilibrium with* $\epsilon \simeq 0$.

PROOF. Consider the allocation $X(t)$ obtained from the fixed point of Theorem 1. $X(t)$ is certainly maximal for all t in T, but we have $1/\omega \, \Sigma \, X(t) \lesssim 1/\omega \, \Sigma \, I(t)$, whereas we require $1/\omega \, \Sigma \, X(t) = 1/\omega \, \Sigma \, I(t)$. Since we know that $p \geq 0$, and $p \cdot X(t) = p \cdot I(t)$, we must have either $1/\omega \, \Sigma \, X^j(t) \simeq 1/\omega \, \Sigma^j(t)$ or $1/\omega \, \Sigma \, X^j(t) \leq 1/\omega \, \Sigma \, I^j(t)$. Suppose the former.

Let $(\nu_1, \ldots, \nu_n) + 1/\omega \, \Sigma \, X(t) = 1/\omega \, \Sigma \, I(t)$. It is important to note that $\nu_i/\omega \simeq 0, i = 1, \ldots, n$. Suppose ν_i a positive integer. If we add one unit of i to the allocation $X(t)$ of each of ν individuals, we will have disturbed the allocations of a negligible set of people. The same reasoning applies if ν_i is negative, in which case we subtract one unit from each of ν_i individuals. After such a perturbation of $X(t)$ for each i, we obtain $Y(t)$, which is an exact allocation—that is, $1/\omega \, \Sigma \, Y(t) = 1/\omega \, \Sigma \, I(t)$. In the above argument we have assumed that it was possible to subtract one unit of any commodity from the chosen traders. If we can subtract only $1/n$ of a unit from each individual, we shall need to perturb the allocations of $n\eta$ individuals. Since $\eta/\omega \simeq 0$, $n\eta/\omega \simeq 0$, for all $n \in N$. Finally, if ν_i is not a positive integer, then we deal instead with $[\nu_i]$, the smallest integer greater than ν_i.

We must show that the perturbed $Y(t)$ does not violate the nonnegativity constraint or go outside our box of size ν, and we shall be done. But Lemma 1 in the appendix to this chapter shows that a positive subset of traders has at least $1/n$ of any given commodity and that almost everyone is at least a finite distance away from the boundary of the box. Hence the procedure stated above is clearly feasible, and we have an ϵ-Rothenberg equilibrium with $\epsilon \simeq 0$. Note that all the "deviants" have been displaced only a finite distance from their optimal bundles and that, by increasing the number of deviants, this discrepancy can be made smaller than any standard real number ϵ. Q.E.D.

Bounding the Absolute Size of Positive Excess Demand

The fixed point of the previous section has provided us with an equilibrium where $1/\omega\, \Sigma\, X'(t) \leq 1/\omega\, \Sigma\, I(t)$. This of course is identical with $\Sigma\, X'(t) \leq \Sigma\, I(t)$. Agents are, however, maximal at bundles $X(t)$, which may not be equal to $X'(t)$. As a result, $\Sigma\, X(t) \neq \Sigma\, I(t)$ in general, and we would like to find some absolute bounds on the size of $|\Sigma\, X(t) - \Sigma\, I(t)|$. The most interesting case is that with $\Sigma\, X'(t) = \Sigma\, I(t)$ because this represents the worst possibility for obtaining large positive excess demands. Thus, we really have to find bounds on $|\Sigma\, X(t) - \Sigma\, X'(t)|$.

By the Shapley-Folkman theorem, at most n individuals have points $X(t) \neq X'(t)$, and as all $X'(t) \epsilon R^n_+$, we can state that

$$|\Sigma\, X(t) - \Sigma\, X'(t)| \leq \max_{t \epsilon \{n\}} |\Sigma\, X(t)| \leq n\, \Sigma \max |X(t)|$$

where $\{n\}$ represents all the distinct n-tuples that can be selected from T. Because $X(t) \subset Bp(t) \leq M$, $\|X(t)\| \leq \nu$ $\therefore$ $|\Sigma\, X'(t)| \leq n\nu$ always. We would like to make the bound on $|\Sigma\, X(t) - \Sigma\, X'(t)|$ a finite number, which is equivalent to bounding $X(t)$ by some finite constant.

As long as initial endowments are permitted to be infinite, it is impossible to restrict $X(t)$ within some finite cube. $\|I(t)\| \leq K$, for some $K \epsilon N$, is thus a necessary condition for obtaining $\|X(t)\| \leq C$ for some $C \epsilon N$. It is not, however, sufficient, because if $p^i \simeq 0$, then $X^i(t)$ can be infinite. We must therefore find conditions under which $p \not\gg 0$, so that $p^j |X^j(t)| \leq p^1 X^1(t) + - + p^n X^n(t) = p \cdot I(t) \leq K$. $\therefore$ $|X^j(t)| \leq K/p^j = C$. So $p \not\gg 0$ will imply $|\Sigma\, X(t) - \Sigma\, X'(t)| \leq nC$, a finite number.

Establishing Strictly Positive Prices

We now turn to finding conditions under which $p \not\gg 0$. We will be using the condition that, at the fixed point, $1/\omega \, \Sigma \, X(t) \leq 1/\omega \, \Sigma \, I(t) \leq K$. Hence it is impossible for there to exist a commodity X^j and a set S^j such that $|S^j|/\omega \simeq 0$ and $|X^j(t)| \geq \theta$, for all t in S_j and for some θ in $*N - N$, that is, almost everyone holds a finite amount of each good. We shall show that $p \not\gg 0$ in ξ_ω, after adding a new assumption to our model. This new assumption relates to a concept called rates of preference increase and requires some exposition.

The marginal rate of substitution (*MRS*) is a ubiquitous concept in partial equilibrium, but it has not been widely accepted in general equilibrium theory because its use requires the existence of differentiable indifference curves and modern general equilibrium theory has frequently dispensed not only with differentiability but also with indifference curves. We now provide a generalization of the *MRS*, called the rates of preference increase (*RPI*), which applies to the more abstract setting but whose use involves the same economic intuition as in the case of the *MRS*. One advantage of the *RPI* is that it is defined across each pair of commodities, just as the *MRS* is, and this makes it potentially very useful in treating economies with an infinite number of commodities.

Let $P(x)$ denote the set of points in R^n preferred to x by an agent and $\bar{P}(x)$ its closure. Because *RPI*'s are defined for pairs of commodities, we shall focus on a particular pair, say commodities 1 and 2, and look at $\bar{P}_{12}(x)$, the projection of $\bar{P}(x)$ on the two-dimensional subspace of goods 1 and 2 with unit vectors e_1 and e_2. Define

$$RPI_{12}(x) \equiv \{\mu/\eta \,|\, (x - \eta e_1 + \mu e_2) \in P(x), \text{ for some } -\infty < \eta < x_1\}.$$

Given that the agent has to lose an amount η of x_1, $RPI_{12}(x)$ tells us how much of x_2, per unit of x_1, will more than compensate for this loss. This definition is not limited to a neighborhood of x, and, as such, is distinguished from the *MRS* even when differentiable indifference curves exist, though the relationship between the two concepts is obvious.

The use of the *RPI* employs the same elementary economic reasoning to be found in introductory microeconomics texts. The *RPI* tells us all the rates at which an individual is willing to give up one commodity for another: the budget set tells us the rates at which an individual can monetarily afford to give up one commodity for another. If the rate he is willing to pay is greater than the rate he is required to pay by the market, he will obviously wish to move and therefore cannot have been in equilibrium. The above reasoning is not dependent upon the budget set being defined by hyperplanes. As an application of the above reasoning, if $RPI(x)$ contains one positive value at x, then p_2 must be positive if p_1 is. This is so because a finite, positive *RPI* indicates that the agent would be better off by exchanging a certain amount of x_1 for an amount of $x_2 = RPI \cdot x_1$. If the price of p_1 is positive and that of $p_2 \simeq 0$, the agent can obtain an infinite amount of x_2 for any finite amount of x_1. Hence the agent cannot be in equilibrium at x. Our fixed-point argument tells us that x is an equilibrium bundle, however; it follows that p_2 must be standardly positive if x_1 is. Of course, this argument holds *a fortiori* if the RPI_{12} equals $+\infty$. In general equilibrium analysis with the assumptions of, say, Debreu (1959), the price of at least one commodity, say 1, is guaranteed to be positive. The above reasoning shows that every commodity that can be linked with commodity 1, by finite *RPI*, perhaps through a chain of intermediate commodities, must also have a positive price; for example, if $RPI_{13}(x)$, $RPI_{35}(x)$, $RPI_{59}(x)$ each contains a positive value, then $p_1 > 0 \Rightarrow p_3 > 0 \Rightarrow p_5 > 0 \Rightarrow p_9 > 0$.

If we are considering linear price systems, the same reasoning tells us that if $RPI_{12}(x)$ is concave to the origin, then x cannot be a point of equilibrium. $RPI_{12}(x)$ contains segments on both sides of x, and so any linear budget set must intersect $P(x)$ and x cannot be a maximal point. Finally, if we wish to have equilibria in which the price of some commodity, say 1, is bounded away from zero, for example, wages must exceed $\bar{w}$, then a sufficient condition for this to be true is that $\bar{w}$ forms an upper bound for $RPI_{1j}(x)$, for all j, for all x.

How can we ensure that preferences will display positive RPI_{ij} for all i, j? Suppose agents' preferences are chosen from a compact subset of the space of strongly monotonic and open standard preferences. By strong monotonicity, if $x \geq y, x \neq y$, then $x \succ y$. By openness of the preferred sets, $x \succ y$ implies that a standard ball of radius r is also preferred to y. Let x and y differ only in the jth component, so that $x = y + \delta e_j$ and $x \succ y$ by strong monotonicity. Then r/δ is certainly a positive RPI_{ij} at y for any i. Strong monotonicity and (standard) openness of the preferred set thus suffice to establish (standardly) positive RPI_{ij} for all pairs of goods and hence the strict (standard) positivity of all prices in equilibrium. This discussion serves to establish Corollary 1.

COROLLARY 1. *If RPI_{ij} is finite for all i, j, $i \neq j$, then $p \gg 0$ at any competitive equilibrium of ξ_w.*

Existence of Equilibrium with Production

In this section the theorem on the existence of a competitive equilibrium is extended to economies with production; that is, in addition to a preference relation over the sets of commodity bundles, each individual has certain productive capabilities, which are summarized by his production set $Y(t)$. At any stated market price p, agent t decides on his most profitable production plan $h(t) \in Y(t)$ (analogously to a consumer's demand). It is first shown that the set of all feasible aggregate consumption plans x—the vectors x, such that $x \leq y + I$, where y is an aggregate production plan and I the total initial endowments—must lie within some bounded set. Hence if an equilibrium exists, then it must lie in a K-cube, where K is finite. The original economy is then replaced by an economy in which the consumption and production sets are bounded by something larger than K, say $K + 1$—we permit consumers and producers only those bundles that lie within the $(K + 1)$-cube. Equilibrium allocations for the bounded economy, if they exist, can be shown to lie strictly in the interior of the $(K + 1)$-cube; this being so, we can claim that the bound did not affect traders' choices, since they chose bundles within the bound anyway. Hence the equilibrium obtained within this suitably bounded economy is actually an equilibrium for the original, unrestricted economy.

If, however, we apply a procedure like that of Debreu (1959) to nonstandard economies with production, the bound K will, in general, be infinite. In fact, it may be that $K/\omega \not\simeq 0$; we, however, must ensure that $K/\omega \simeq 0$ in order to apply our theorems on the convexity of the average sum of a large number of sets. We therefore approach our problem somewhat differently than Debreu.[3]

In our assumptions about the productivity capacity of the economy, we shall follow Hildenbrand (1974) in assuming that the joint productive capacity of a coalition is the sum of the productive capacities of all its members. As observed by Hildenbrand, this formulation includes as a special case economies with a finite number of producers. A production set correspondence Y, from ϕ, the set of coalitions, into the commodity space, R_n, is said to be *additive* if

$$Y\left(\bigcup_{i=1}^{\nu} R_i\right) = \sum_{i=1}^{\nu} Y(R_i)$$

for every collection (R_i) of ν pairwise-disjoint members of ϕ. Since individuals are members of ϕ, we can define unambiguously each individual's income from production when prices are given by the vector p as $\Pi(t, p) = \sup\{p \cdot y \mid y \in Y(t)\}$.

The reason for assuming additivity of the production correspondence is to ensure disaggregation of total profits into profit shares for individual producers.

3. Unlike Debreu, I do not assume convexity of preferences.

Unlike Hildenbrand, who assumes that all individual production sets are convex and contain the origin, we will assume only that the individual production sets contain the origin—that is, producers are not forced to produce at a loss. We will assume that the aggregate production set Y is closed and convex. Since we have an infinite number of producers, we can obtain the approximate convexity of the average aggregate production set, approximate to within an infinitesimal, by bounding production possibilities within some sufficiently small cube—for example, of size ν such that $\nu/\omega \simeq 0$. This is not adequate for our purposes because in the presence of increasing returns to scale, individual producers will always choose to be at the boundary of our cube, and unless we can show that their preferred points are strictly interior to our bounding cube, we cannot claim that our bounded equilibrium is a true equilibrium. Hence we are forced to assume that all individual returns are eventually nonincreasing.

For any production vector y, the inputs are denoted as negative quantities, and the outputs are denoted as positive quantities. For proving existence, we will require that some assumptions are made on the productivity of the economy. The reason for such assumptions is the necessity of requiring that all traders are "small" in relation to the size of the economy. When we are concerned only with exchange, this smallness is adequately captured by the condition that $I(t)/\omega \simeq 0$. In the case of production, however, this condition is inadequate. Consider an agent who possesses only one unit of labor to start with, but who is so productive that he can produce ω^n units of any consumption good he wishes. This consumer can be considered to start off with an infinite amount of every commodity, and he is anything but negligible in our model.

There are two reasons why this problem does not arise in standard economies. First, the measure used on the space of consumers differs from the metric used in commodity space. Even if a single consumer has "infinite productivity" in a measure-theoretic economy, such negligible sets can be safely ignored. In the nonstandard framework, the measure on consumers is usually counting measure. Second, the requirement that the aggregate production possibility set be convex, together with the postulate "no outputs without inputs," suffices to bound the productivity of inputs at all points, except possibly the origin. In the nonstandard case, convexity is no help because in the example given above, we could have a production possibility set that is a cone, whose projections along each output have slope ω^n.

The economy will be formally specified as follows: A nonstandard economy with production, ξ_ω, consists of an internal set of traders $T = \{1, \ldots, \omega\}$ with $\omega \in {}^*N - N$. The economy will be completely specified by assigning to each trader an initial endowment $I(t)$, a consumption set X_t, preferences $\}_t$ on X_t, a production set, which shall be $*R^n$ for all traders, and a production technology Y_t. In what follows, all assignments are assumed to be internal.

Endowments. It will be assumed that $1/\omega\ \Sigma\ I(t) \gg 0$, and that $I(t)/\omega \simeq 0$ for all t. We will therefore have $1/\omega\ \Sigma\ I(t) \leq \nu e$, with $\nu/\omega \simeq 0$.

Consumption. Each consumption set X_t is assumed to be convex, closed, and bounded below. There exists a continuous, transitive, locally nonsatiated ordering of X_t, denoted by $\}_t$, for the tth agent.

Production. The assignment of production technologies to individuals, which will be correspondences denoted by Y_t, is assumed to be additive over coalitions—that is, $Y_S = \Sigma_{t \in S}\ Y_t$, for any internal coalition set $S \subseteq T$. Each Y_t contains the origin. The aggregate production possibility set $Y = \Sigma_T\ Y_t$ is assumed to be closed, convex, and to permit free disposal—that is, $y_1 \in Y$, $y_2 \leq y_1$, implies $y_2 \in Y$. Inputs are denominated as negative and outputs as positive quantities. If y_i denotes the maximal input, and y_0 the maximal output, in a production vector, y, we shall assume that $y_0/|y_i| \leq \gamma$, for some suitably chosen $\gamma \in *N - N$.

Let $\Pi(t, p)$ denote the share of profits of the tth trader at prices p. This is well defined, since the production sets are assumed additive. A *competitive equilibrium* for ξ_ω is said to exist if there are $p \in S$, $X(t) \in X_t$, $y(t) \in Y_t$, for all t in T.

(a) $X(t)$ is a maximal point for $\}_t$, in the tth trader's budget set $B_p(t) = \{X \in *R^n | p \cdot X \leq p \cdot I(t) + \Pi(t, p)\}$.

(b) $p \cdot y(t) = \max p \cdot y$, for all $y \in Y_t$.

(c) $1/\omega\ \Sigma\ X(t) \leq 1/\omega\, y(t) + 1/\omega\ \Sigma\ I(t)$.

THEOREM 2. *There exists a competitive equilibrium for* ξ_ω.

Before turning to the proof, it may be helpful to motivate the bound needed for applying a fixed-point theorem.

We need a cube of size ν that is infinitely larger than the maximal value of $\|I(t)\|$ (where $\|-\|$ denotes the sup norm); we need all feasible production bundles to lie within the ν-cube; this necessitates $\nu \geq m\gamma$; we also require that all outputs within the cube be producible by inputs chosen from within the cube, and this leads to $\nu \geq m\gamma^2$. Finally, ν must be "small" relative to ω, so that Loeb's theorem applies—that is, $m\gamma^2/\omega \simeq 0$, a requirement that makes it clear that m, γ, and ω cannot be independently chosen.

PROOF OF THEOREM 2. We begin by suitably bounding commodity space. Set the bound $\nu = m\gamma^2$, where $m = \max_T \|I(t)\|$ and γ, the bound on producibility, is chosen such that $m\gamma^2/\omega \simeq 0$. This is always possible for suitable choice of $\gamma \in *N - N$. Let $S = S_\eta$ as defined earlier.

Define

$M = \{X \in {}^*R^n \mid X \leq \nu e,\ \nu \in {}^*N - N\}$,

$Bp(t) = \{X \in {}^*R^n \mid p \cdot X \leq p \cdot I(t) + \Pi(t, p)\}$,

$Cp(t) = Bp(t) \cap M$,

$$Dp(t) = \begin{cases} \{X \subseteq Bp(t) \text{ such that } X \text{ is maximal in } Cp(t)\} \text{ if } p \cdot I(t) > 0, \\ \{Cp(t)\} \text{ if } p \cdot I(t) = 0. \end{cases}$$

$\hat{Y}_t = Y_t \cap M$,

$$\hat{Y} = \frac{1}{\omega} \Sigma \hat{Y}_t,$$

$\alpha : S \to M,\ \alpha(p) = \{y \in \hat{Y} \mid p \cdot y \geq p \cdot y',\ \forall y' \in \hat{Y}\}$,

$$\psi : S \to M,\ \psi(p) = \left\{x \in {}^*R_n \mid \text{assignment } X(t),\ X(t) \in Dp(t) \text{ such that } x = \frac{1}{\omega} \Sigma X(t)\right\} \text{—that is, } \psi(p) = \frac{1}{\omega} \Sigma D_p(t).$$

$$\phi : M \times M \to S; \text{ define } \frac{1}{\omega} \Sigma I(t) \equiv I, \text{ then } \phi(x, y)$$

$$= \{p \in P \mid p \cdot (x - y - I) \geq q \cdot (x - y - I) \text{ for all } q \in S\}.$$

$\hat{\psi} : S \to M$, the Q-convex hull of $\psi(p)$.

Since ϕ is the set of maximizers of a linear function over a compact set, the transfer of Theorem 5.5 applies, and the set of maximizers is nonempty with the maximal profit a continuous function of prices. As a result, (a) Π is a convex-valued, upper-semicontinuous correspondence, (b) the budget sets $Bp(t)$ are continuous functions of p, and therefore, (c) by a transfer of Theorem 5.5 once again, each member of the correspondence $\hat{\psi}(p)$ is nonempty, internal, and upper-semicontinuous. The aggregate $\hat{\psi}(p)$ is thus also nonempty, internal, and upper-semicontinuous. It is also convex by the nonstandard analogue of Lyapunov's theorem, Theorem 5.1.

The correspondence $\theta = \phi \times \alpha \times \hat{\psi}$ is thus a convex-valued, upper-semicontinuous mapping from $M \times M \times P$, which is a Q-compact, Q-convex set, into itself. By transfer of Kakutani's theorem, it will have a fixed point $(p, y, \hat{x})$.

There will exist an assignment $X(t)$ such that $\hat{x} \simeq x = 1/\omega\, \Sigma X(t)$ and $X(t) \in Dp(t)$. $X(t) \in Dp(t) \subseteq Cp(t) \subseteq Bp(t)$ implies $p \cdot X(t) \leq p \cdot I(t) +$

$\pi(t, p)$. Suppose that $p \cdot I(t) + \Pi(t, p) - p \cdot X(t) = \epsilon$, $\epsilon > 0$—that is, the maximal bundle lies strictly within the budget set.

By local nonsatiation there will exist $X'(t)$ in an n-dimensional ϵ-ball around $X'(t)$ such that $X'(t) \succ X(t)$. Since $X'(t)$ is in the ϵ-neighborhood of $X(t)$, we will also have $p \cdot X'(t) \leq p \cdot I(t) + \Pi(t, p)$—that is, $X'(t)$ is in the budget set and preferred to $X(t)$. This contradicts the maximality of $X(t)$. Therefore, $p \cdot X(t) = p \cdot I(t) + \Pi(t, p)$ for all t.

Let $b = (x - y - I)$. Since $p \cdot X(t) = p \cdot I(t) + \Pi(t, p)$, it follows that $p \cdot b = 0$. By definition of ϕ, $(\forall q \in S)(p \cdot b > q \cdot b)$—that is, $0 > q \cdot b$.

Set $q \simeq e_i$, $i = 1, \ldots, n$. Then, by mimicking the proof for the case of an exchange economy, $0 \gtrsim e_i b = b^i$—that is, the excess demand for every good is either negative or infinitesimal.

If we can now show that after removing the constraint of the cube, the same bundles $X(t)$, $y(t)$ are still maximal, we shall be done.[4] Our budget sets were chosen so that they lay wholly within the cube, so we have only to worry about production.

As $1/\omega \, \Sigma \, y(t) = y \in \hat{Y}$, we must have $y \leq m\gamma e$, by the assumption of bounded producibility. Therefore, y is strictly within our ν-cube. Suppose there exists y^* with $p \cdot y^* > p \cdot y$, $y^* \in Y$. As Y is convex, $\lambda y^* + (1 - \lambda)y \in Y$, for all λ between 0 and 1. As y is interior to $\hat{Y}$, there exists $\bar{\lambda}$ such that $\bar{\lambda} y^* + (1 - \bar{\lambda})y \in \hat{Y}$. But $p \cdot (\bar{\lambda} y^* + (1 - \bar{\lambda} y)) > p \cdot y$, contradicting the maximality of y in $\hat{Y}$. By (3.4.1) of Debreu (1959), $y(t)$ is maximal in Y_t. Q.E.D.

REMARK. The robustness of our proof may be seen by noting that very little will have to be altered to deal with nonadditive correspondences. The chief difficulty with nonadditive production correspondences, as pointed out in the pioneering work of Dieter Sondermann (1975), lies in showing the continuity of the profit-allocation function with respect to prices. The two profit-allocation mechanisms proposed in this case are the core and the Shapley value. In almost all cases hitherto discussed, both these allocative mechanisms are continuous functions of prices in finite economies. They will, therefore, also be continuous in the nonstandard economy by "transfer." The above proof, without modification of our arguments, will then prove the existence of an equilibrium in Sondermann's sense for all cases when the profit function is a continuous function of prices in finite economies.

4. It is this step that prevents our using a nonconvex aggregate production set; if we did so, the optimal $Y(t)$'s could all lie on the boundary of the cube, for arbitrarily large cubes, and we would be unable to complete the proof.

Appendix

As the proof of Lemma 1 uses the idea of a comprehensive enlargement, I have provided it as an appendix. I suspect that a proof without using comprehensive enlargements can also be found.

LEMMA 1. *Let* $X(t)$ *be an internal function from* T *into* $^*R^n$ *such that* $X(t) \leq \nu$, *for all* $t \in T$, *where* $\nu^2 = m\omega$ *and* $m/\nu \simeq 0$. *Assume further that*

(i) $\dfrac{X(t)}{\omega} \simeq 0$ *for all* t *in* T.

(ii) $m \geq \dfrac{1}{\omega} \sum_{T/V} X(t) \not\gg 0. \qquad \left(V \subseteq T \,\middle|\, \dfrac{|V|}{\omega} \simeq 0\right).$

It is then true that

(a) *If* $S_n = \left\{t \in T \,|\, X(t) \geq \dfrac{1}{n}\right\}$, *then* $|S_n|/\omega \not\simeq 0$, *for some* $n \in N$.

(b) *If* $S'_k = \{t \in T \,|\, X(t) \geq \nu - k,\, k \in N\}$, *then* $|S'_k|/\omega \simeq 0$, *for all* $k \in N$.

PROOF. (a) Suppose $\mu(S_n) = |S_n|/\omega \simeq 0$ for all n. Since we are working in a comprehensive enlargement, we can extend $\{S_n, \mu(S_n)\}$ in internal fashion up to some $\gamma \in {}^*N - N$—that is, there exists S_γ with $\mu(S_\gamma) \simeq 0$. But then

$$\frac{1}{\omega} \sum_{T/S_\gamma} X(t) \simeq 0,$$

which contradicts our assumption that

$$\frac{1}{\omega} \sum_{T/V} X(t) \not\gg 0, \qquad (V \subseteq T,\ |V|/\omega \simeq 0).$$

Hence there exists n such that $\mu(S_n) \not\simeq 0$.

(b) Suppose

$$\mu(S'_k) = \frac{|S'_k|}{\omega} \not\simeq 0.$$

Then

$$\frac{1}{\omega} \sum_B X(t) \geq \frac{1}{\omega} \sum_{S'_k} X(t) \geq \frac{|S'_k|}{\omega} \cdot (\nu - k), \qquad \text{but}$$

$$\frac{1}{\omega} \sum_B X(t) \leq m' \text{—that is,}$$

$$m \geq \frac{1}{\omega} \sum_B X(t) \geq \frac{|S'_k|}{\omega} \cdot (\nu - k), \text{ a contradiction since } \frac{m}{\nu} \simeq 0.$$

This concludes the proofs.

III

EDGEWORTH'S CONJECTURE

Chapters 8, 9, and 10 deal with various versions of Edgeworth's conjecture on the equivalence of core and competitive equilibria in large economies. Chapters 8 and 9 prove the validity of this conjecture for different definitions of "core" and "competitive equilibria," and chapter 10 deals with the validity of the conjecture when large traders, in a sense to be made precise, are allowed. Chapter 8 should be tackled first by the reader new to this literature. I have made an effort to explain the intuition as well as to guide the reader through the proof of the principal result in chapter 8.

To minimize notation, I have sometimes referred to the version of core and competitive equilibrium used in each chapter simply as the core *and* the competitive equilibrium. *The reader should exercise some care in comparing definitions across chapters. A guide to the various possibilities is provided on page 88.*

8

Core Equivalence Theorems

Why do we expect cores to be priced out? The following intuitive argument (essentially attributable to Debreu and Scarf, 1963) may help us to see why core allocations in large economies will tend to be associated with price systems. Consider an economy such as the one discussed in chapter 1, in which there are two types of traders, A and B, and for which the allocation (X_A, X_B) is a core allocation. Form the sets $G_A = P_A(X_A) - W_A$ and $G_B = P_B(X_B) - W_B$, which consist of the set of points preferred to the core allocation minus the initial endowment, that is, the *net* bundles preferred to X_A and X_B. As a result, $y_A \in G_A$ and $y_B \in G_B$ will block (X_A, X_B) if $y_A + y_B = 0$ (figure 11).

Suppose now that (X_A, X_B) cannot be priced out, so that there exists a hyperplane which intersects both G_A and G_B.[1] Such a hyperplane provides just the means for blocking by movements from the origin 0 to y_A and y_B. Obviously the vectors $0y_A$ and $0y_B$ satisfy $0y_A + 0y_B = 0$, so they represent feasible and preferred movements from (X_A, X_B). The intersection of a hyperplane with both sets G_A and G_B thus provides us with a simple way of checking out whether there are feasible ways of entering the (net) preferred-to sets.

What happens, however, if the sets G_A and G_B are not as conveniently placed as in the previous diagram so that $0y_A \neq -0y_B$? At this point, enlarging the size of the economy comes into play. Suppose the points z_A and

1. If X_A and X_B can be priced out, this means that there exists a price vector p such that $p \cdot X_A = p \cdot W_A$, $p \cdot X_B = p \cdot W_B$, and X_A, X_B are maximal elements in their budget sets. With convexity, maximality implies that the budget set is tangent to the preferred sets of X_A and X_B. Hence, if (X_A, X_B) can be priced out, there must exist a hyperplane tangent to both G_A and G_B at X_A and X_B respectively.

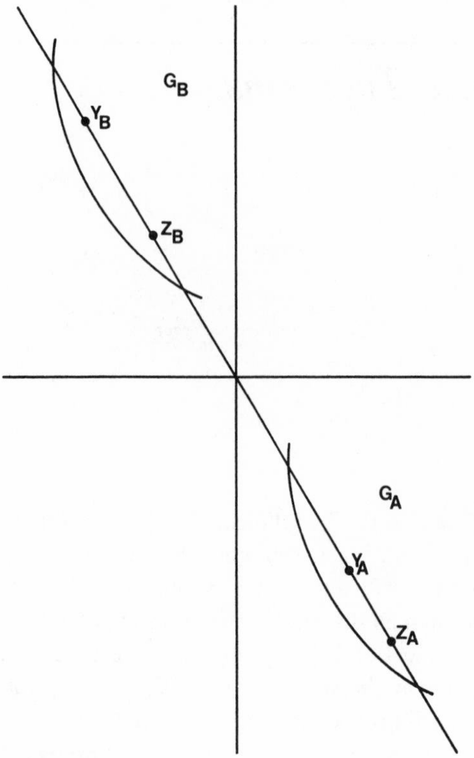

Figure 11. Net preferred-to sets that intersect a hyperplane, indicating blocking is possible.

z_B are as in figure 11. In this case we add K_B traders of type B until $K_B z_B + z_A = 0$. If this does not work out, we add K_A traders of type A until $K_B z_B + K_A z_A = 0$, and so on. If all coordinates of z_A and z_B are rational, the existence of K_A and K_B is clear from the existence of a common multiple for any finite set of numbers. The general case follows by using only points with rational coordinates to approximate any given point.

Generalizing the intuition of the above argument, we see that if there exists any subset S of traders for whom a hyperplane through the origin intersects $\Sigma_S\, G_j(X_j^*)$, $j \in S$, that coalition S becomes a candidate for blocking the proposed allocation. It follows that, for any allocation $(X_1^*, \ldots, X_T^*)$ to be in the core, we must have

$$\sum_S G_j(X_j^*) \cap 0 = \emptyset, \qquad \forall S \subseteq T. \tag{*}$$

This equation can be expressed more compactly if we define $G \equiv \Sigma_T\, [G_j(X_j^*) \cup \{0\}]$, where we allow 0 in each term so as to accommodate those agents in $T - S$ for any coalition S. The condition (*) for the allocation $(X_1^*, \ldots, X_T^*)$ not to be blocked is now[2]

$$G \cap 0 = \emptyset. \qquad (**)$$

To be able to form a price system we must show (1) that G is either convex or very nearly convex, so that a separating hyperplane distinguishes points of G from 0, and (2) that this separating hyperplane has the properties of a price vector, that is, it is nonnegative, and that it defines a budget set for each individual. These two points form the heart of any equivalence proof.

Except for trivial cases, $G_j \cup \{0\}$ is never convex, regardless of the convexity of G_j, so convexity of preferences is of little help in core equivalence theorems. A more important consequence is that G, the sum of $G_j \cup \{0\}$, is never entirely convex, hence cannot be exactly separated from 0. This implies that the equivalence theorem will be only an approximation result.[3]

Since core allocations become more like competitive equilibria as the number of agents increases, what happens if we have an infinite number of traders? Let us write out the core equivalence result formally as follows, where $\zeta_e(\xi_k)$ denotes the set of competitive equilibria of the economy ξ_k and $\zeta(\xi_k)$ denotes the core of the same economy:

$$(\forall \epsilon > 0)(\exists k \in N)(\| \zeta(\xi_k) - \zeta_e(\xi_k) \| < \epsilon).$$

This tells us that we can make the set of core allocations and competitive equilibria approach arbitrarily close to each other by choosing a suitably large economy. It does *not* tell us that there exists a large enough finite economy in which the core equals competitive equilibria; there is no sudden equality, just better and better approximations. What, then, can we expect of economies with an infinite number of traders? If we demand that infinite economies be modeled in such a way that *exact* equality holds between the set of core and competitive equilibria, then infinite economies will display behavior that is, so to speak, discontinuously different from the behavior of finite economies. There is nothing inherently wrong with this, but if our eventual goal is to throw light on large finite economies by examining the properties of infinite economies, such a model achieves our goal indirectly. Alternatively, we could model an infinite economy in such

2. The condition (**) will be expressed as $[\int G_j \cup \{0\}] \cap 0 = \emptyset$ if we wish to work with integrals instead of sums.

3. If we try to use (*) instead of (**), then each sum of the form $\Sigma\, G_j, j \in S \subseteq T$, is convex if each G_j is convex. Our difficulty now becomes that of showing that the entire collection of these convex sums has a *common* separating hyperplane.

a way that in an economy with an infinitely large number of traders the core and competitive equilibria are infinitesimally close to each other. For such models the core equivalence theorem would read

$$(\forall \epsilon > 0)(\exists k \in N)(\| \zeta(\xi_k) - \zeta_e(\xi_k) \| < \epsilon), \qquad (***)$$

where ϵ is now an infinitesimal and k is an infinite integer. Note that the structure of the corresponding theorem for finite economies is preserved exactly. As a result the transition from finite to infinite economies is easy. The first way of modeling infinite economies uses measure theory, the second nonstandard analysis.

The above discussion should have also pointed out that an *exact* equality between the core and competitive equilibria is not to be had, regardless of the size of the economy. (This is obvious from (***) for the nonstandard model; it is equally true but not so obvious for the measure-theoretic model, as will be pointed out in chapter 12.) In fact, an elegant example of Lloyd Shapley's shows that the rate at which the core converges to the competitive equilibria can be arbitrarily slow (Shapley, 1975).

Since the exact equivalence does not hold even in infinite economies we must be satisfied with approximations, and we have to ask ourselves what concepts we wish to approximate. We can form approximate cores by changing our requirements for

A. What sorts of coalitions form permissible blocking coalitions.
B. The resources that such blocking coalitions are permitted to use.
C. The extent to which a proposed allocation must be better than a given allocation for the proposed allocation to be an improvement.

Restrictions on A and B alter feasibility requirements, and C alters optimality. When all commodities are divisible they are largely interchangeable, as we shall see later.

If $X(t)$ denotes a core allocation, S a blocking coalition, and $Y(t)$ a proposed allocation that blocks $X(t)$, our alternatives can be depicted as

A. (i) $S \neq \emptyset$ (ii) $\dfrac{|S|}{\omega} \neq 0.$

B. (i) $\dfrac{1}{\omega} \Sigma X(t) \lesssim \dfrac{1}{\omega} \Sigma I(t)$ (ii) $\dfrac{1}{\omega} \Sigma X(t) \lnsim \dfrac{1}{\omega} \Sigma I(t).$

C. (i) $Y \succ_t X$ (ii) $Y \succ\!\succ_t X.$

This leads to a total of eight possibilities. Those involving A(i), however, are not very interesting—in an economy with $10^{10^{10}}$ traders, the dissatisfaction of three individuals is not very disturbing. So we are left with four possibilities. Of these, B(i) and C(i) will be dealt with in this chapter, and B(ii) and C(i) will be discussed in chapter 9. Because C(ii) is a strong condition to impose, we shall ignore it until chapter 12. The definition of core that we shall use here will say X is in the *core* if there does not exist a nonnegligible set of traders S and an allocation Y such that, for all t in S, $X(t) \succ_t Y(t)$, and

$$\frac{1}{\omega} \sum_S Y(t) \lesssim \frac{1}{\omega} \sum_S I(t).$$

We now formally define the nonstandard economy.

A *nonstandard exchange economy* consists of a pair of functions I and P, where $I:T \to {}^*R^n$ and $P:T \to \mathcal{P}({}^*R^n \times {}^*R^n)$ and $\mathcal{P}({}^*R^n)$ denotes the power set of ${}^*R^n$.

We shall denote the functions I and P respectively as $[I(t)]_{t=1}^{\omega}$ and $(\succ_t)_{t=1}^{\omega}$, where $I(t)$ is to be interpreted as the initial endowment of trader t and $\succ_t$ as his preference relation over ${}^*R^n$. We will assume that ξ_ω has the following properties:

(A.1) The function indexing the initial endowments, $I(t)$ is internal.

(A.2) $\frac{1}{\omega} \sum_{t \in T} I(t) \not\simeq\!\!\gg 0.$

(A.3) The relation, Q, where $Q = \{(t, \succ_t) \mid t \in T, \succ_t \subseteq {}^*R^n \times {}^*R^n\}$ is internal. For all t:

(α) $\succ_t$ is irreflexive.

(β) If $x \gg y$ then $x \succ_t y$.

We shall need the following concepts for this limited economy, ξ_ω.

(D.1) An *assignment* is an internal function from T into ${}^*R^n_+$.

(D.2) An *allocation* is an assignment Y such that

$$\frac{1}{\omega} \sum_{t \in T} Y(t) = \frac{1}{\omega} \sum_{t \in T} I(t).$$

(D.3) A *coalition* S is an internal subset of T. It is said to be *negligible* if $|S|/\omega \simeq 0$.

(D.4) An allocation Y *blocks* an allocation X if there exists a nonnegligible coalition S such that

(a) $Y(t) \succ_t X(t) (\forall t \in S)$ (b) $\frac{1}{\omega} \sum_S Y(t) \lesssim \frac{1}{\omega} \sum_S I(t)$

(D.5) An allocation Y is in the *core* if there exists no allocation that blocks it.

(D.6) A *price system* p is a vector in $*R^n_+$ such that $p > 0$.

(D.7) The tth trader's *budget set*, $B_p(t)$, is $\{x \in *R^n_+ | p \cdot x \lesssim p \cdot I(t)\}$.

(D.8) y is said to be *maximal* in $B_p(t)$ if $y \in B_p(t)$ and $x \succ y \Rightarrow p \cdot x \gtrsim p \cdot y$

(D.9) An ϵ-*equilibrium* is defined as a pair (p, X) where p is a price system and X an allocation such that $X(t)$ is maximal for all but a negligible set of traders.

THEOREM 1. *If ξ_ω satisfies* (A.1) *to* (A.4), *then corresponding to any allocation X in the core, there exists a price system p such that (p, X) is an ϵ-equilibrium of ξ_ω.*

PROOF. To emphasize the closeness with which the proof follows our intuition, the proof is broken down into four steps, A, B, C, and D.

A. Step A is the first of the two crucial steps mentioned earlier and serves to establish the S-convexity of the aggregate preferred-to set.

Let X be in the core of ξ_ω.

Let $\ell = \max_T \max_i I_i(t)$. ℓ will serve to bound the preferred-to sets.

As $I(t)$ is integrable, $\frac{\ell}{\omega} \simeq 0$.

Pick $\ell' \in *N - N$ so that $\frac{\ell'\ell}{\omega} \simeq 0$.

Set $\nu = \ell'\ell$ and define,

$$F_\nu(t) = \{z(t)\, *R^n | z(t) \succ X(t) \wedge z(t) \leq \nu e\}$$

$$G_\nu(t) = \{F_\nu(t) - I(t)\} \cup \{0\}$$

$$G_\nu = \frac{1}{\omega} \Sigma\, G_\nu(t).$$

By monotonicity of preferences, $x(t) = X(t) + e \succ_t X(t)$. So each $F_\nu(t)$ is nonempty and so is L_ν. By choice of ν each $G_\nu(t)/\omega \simeq 0$.

By Brown's theorem on the S-convexity of infinitesimal sums, G_ν is S-convex.

B. Step B shows that the origin is not interior to the aggregate preferred-to set, that is, $0 \notin \text{int } G_\nu$, and hence can be separated from the convex hull of G_ν.

Suppose $0 \in \text{int } G_\nu$

$$h(t) \quad G_\nu(t) \quad \text{and} \quad \frac{1}{\omega} \Sigma\, h(t) \ll 0.$$

Let $U = \{t \,|\, h(t) \neq 0\}$.

If $\dfrac{|U|}{\omega} \simeq 0$, neglect U.

If $\dfrac{|U|}{\omega} \not\simeq 0$, define $Z(t) = h(t) + I(t)$ for $t \in U$.

As $h(t) \in G_\nu(t)$, $Z(t) = h(t) + I(t) \succ_t X(t)$.

As $\dfrac{|U|}{\omega} \not\simeq 0$, $Z(t)$ blocks $X(t)$ via the coalition U.

This contradicts our assumption that X is a core allocation. As L_ν is S-convex, $0 \notin \text{int } G_\nu$ implies that $0 \notin S\text{-int } Q \text{ con } G_\nu$, or, $bdy(Q\text{-con } G_\nu) \simeq 0$. So our infinitesimally convex set of preferred-to points must be within an infinitely small neighborhood of zero. Hence G_ν can be almost separated from 0 by a hyperplane.

$$\exists p \neq 0 \text{ s.t. } p \cdot x \gtrsim 0, \qquad \forall x \in (Q\text{-con } G_\nu).$$

Since G_ν is S-convex

$$\Rightarrow p \cdot x \gtrsim 0, \qquad \forall x \in G_\nu$$

C. The conclusion of step B was that the aggregate sum of preferred-to points in G_ν is infeasible in value; in step C this will be shown to imply that, for almost all traders, preferred-to points cost more than their initial endowment (give or take an infinitesimal). The first step lies in finding a standard price vector approximating p.

Let $p = {}^\circ p + \tilde{p}$ where $\tilde{p} \simeq 0$.

As $\tilde{p} \cdot x \simeq 0$ for all x in any finite cube, it follows by Robinson's Lemma that

$\tilde{p} \cdot x \simeq 0$ for all $x \in G_{\nu'}$ for some $\nu' \in {}^*N - N$.

Set $\nu'' = \min\{\nu, \nu'\}$

Suppose there exists a nonnegligible set of traders B such that ${}^\circ p \cdot z(t) \lesssim {}^\circ p \cdot I(t)$ for all t in B.

Select $h(t)$ such that $h(t) = z(t) - I(t)$ for all t in B and $h(t) = 0$, for $t \in T/B$.

Then

$$^\circ p \cdot \left(\frac{1}{\omega} \sum_T h(t)\right) = {}^\circ p \cdot \left(\frac{1}{\omega} \sum_B h(t)\right) \lesssim 0$$

contradicting ${}^\circ p \cdot x \gtrsim 0$ for all $x \in G_{\nu''}$.

D. Finally, $X(t)$ is shown to lie in the budget set defined by ${}^{o}p$, that is,

${}^{o}p \cdot (X(t) - I(t)) \simeq 0$ for almost all traders, and ${}^{o}p \geq 0$. Hence ${}^{o}p$ will be the price vector we desire.

Since $X(t) + \delta e \succ X(t)$ for any $\delta > 0$, it follows that ${}^{o}p \cdot X(t) \gtrsim {}^{o}p \cdot I(t)$ for all traders.

On the other hand, if ${}^{o}p \cdot X(t) \gtrsim\!\!\!\!\!/\;\; {}^{o}p \cdot I(t)$ for a nonnegligible set of traders, then we will have

$${}^{o}p \cdot \frac{1}{\omega} \sum_{T} X(t) \gtrsim\!\!\!\!\!/\;\; {}^{o}p \cdot \frac{1}{\omega} \sum_{T} I(t),$$

which contradicts

$$\frac{1}{\omega} \Sigma\, X(t) = \frac{1}{\omega} \Sigma\, I(t).$$

Suppose some component of ${}^{o}p$, say ${}^{o}p_1 < 0$.

As ${}^{o}p$ is standard, ${}^{o}p_1 \lesssim\!\!\!\!\!/\;\; 0$.

For any trader τ, $X(\tau) + (\nu'', \delta, \ldots, \delta) \succ X(\tau)$, for any finite $\delta > 0$. Hence

$$p \cdot X(\tau) = p_1 \nu'' + \left(\sum_{2}^{n} p_i\right)\delta \gtrsim p \cdot I(\tau).$$

But $p_1 \cdot \nu'' < 0$ and $(p_1 \cdot \nu'' - \delta)$ is infinite, so a contradiction is reached if we pick τ such that $I(\tau)$ is finite. Q.E.D.

It was pointed out in chapter 6, on Pareto-optimality, that the notion of price decentralization was hard to interpret with preferences that were not strictly convex. Only with strictly convex preferences can we ensure that the commodity bundles freely chosen by individuals are precisely those bundles they are required to choose by our equilibrium condition. Theorem 2, by Robert M. Anderson (1982), shows that, in the presence of strong convexity, core allocations are just as well-behaved as Pareto-optimal allocations.

Preferences are said to be *strongly convex* if they satisfy the following condition: if $x \neq y$, then either $[(x + y)/2] \succ x$ or $[(x + y)/2] \succ y$. The preferences are not otherwise assumed to be transitive or complete.

THEOREM 2. *Let agents' preferences be chosen from a compact subset of the set of strictly convex preferences. If X is a core allocation and p is the price vector that decentralizes X, then* $p \gg\!\!\!\!\!/\;\; 0$. *If* $Y(t)$ *maximizes* $\succ_t$ *subject to* $p \cdot x \lesssim p \cdot I(t)$ *then* $Y(t) \simeq X(t)$.

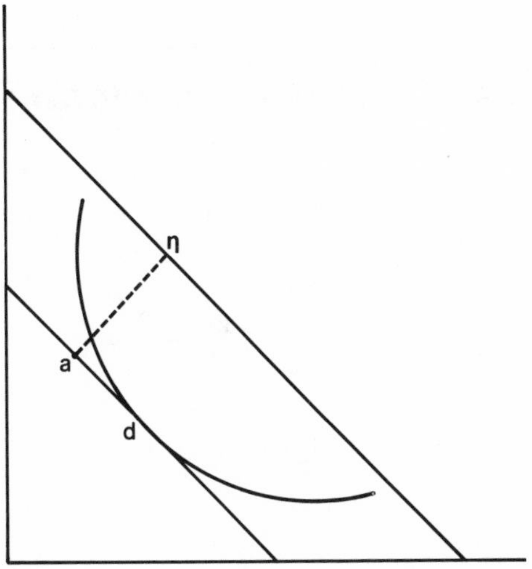

Figure 12. Strict convexity, which implies (infinitesimal) optimality.

PROOF. Given X in the core, a price vector p that decentralizes X is given by Theorem 1. We also know that every component p_i either equals 0 or is standardly positive. Strict convexity, however, permits only $p_i \gtrsim 0$ (with $\not\simeq$).

Suppose $p_i = 0$ for some i.
$X(t) + e_i \succ X(t)$.

By continuity, a neighborhood of $X(t) + e_i$ is also preferred to $X(t)$
$z(t) = X(t) + (-\delta, \ldots, -\delta, 1, -\delta, \ldots, -\delta) \succ X(t)$.

$$p \cdot z(t) = p \cdot X(t) - \delta(\sum_{j \neq i} p_j) < p \cdot X(t),$$

contradicting $p \cdot z(t) \gtrsim p \cdot X(t)$ for $z(t) \succ X(t)$.
If $Y(t)$ maximizes $\succ_t$ subject to $p \cdot x \lesssim p \cdot I(t)$ we must show that $Y(t) \simeq X(t)$ (see figure 12).
Let d be the point of tangency for $\succ_t$ and a budget line $p \cdot I(t) - \epsilon$ for some $\epsilon \simeq 0$. It will suffice if we can show that if η is preferred to d and $p \cdot \eta = p \cdot I(t) + \delta$ for some $\delta \simeq 0$, then $\eta \simeq d$. Draw the plane through η and d. The argument can now be completed in this two-dimensional plane. The angle $ad\eta$ is standard by strict convexity of $\succ_t$ and the fact that $\succ_t$ is standard. The distance $a\eta$ is $\simeq 0$ since a and η lie on hyperplanes each of which is infinitesimally close to $p \cdot I(t)$. Hence $\eta d \simeq 0$.

9

Cores with Costs of Coalition Formation

The object of this chapter is to show that under certain conditions the core allocations of a large but finite economy can be sustained as approximate competitive equilibria even when there are costs associated with the formation of coalitions.[1] It is part of conventional wisdom that core theory suffers by assuming a world of costless coalition formation. K. J. Arrow and F. H. Hahn, for example, write that perhaps the most important qualification to the core-equivalence results is "the neglect of costs of coalition formation. Actually, it is probably the fact that the costs of forming coalitions of different kinds of individuals are different rather than the mere existence of bargaining costs that is of critical importance. . . . If the costs of bargaining are not uniform for different coalitions, then indeed quite different results may prevail (1971:186).

This chapter takes a step in addressing these important points. We show that if small coalitions face small costs of coalition formation and if their members are not very dissimilar, then core allocations can be priced out as approximate competitive equilibria. The following section defines the various restricted cores that have appeared in the literature and illustrates by diagrams some of our notions. The next section defines a general core with costs of coalition formation, which encompasses most of the cores in the first section. Edgeworth's conjecture is then reformulated to apply to our cores. Finally, proofs of our results are provided.

1. This chapter is based on an earlier Johns Hopkins Working Paper with M. Ali Khan (1977), but the proof is very different. The substance of our results was announced in Khan and Rashid (1978).

Restricted Cores

We begin by considering an economy with n goods and k traders. We shall denote such an economy by E_k^n and its set of traders by T_k. Each trader t in T_k has an *initial endowment*, $I(t)$ in R_+^n, and a *preference ordering*, $\succ_t$, defined on $R_+^n \times R_+^n$. For any pair of commodity bundles, x, y in R_+^n, we shall read $x \succ_t y$ as "x is preferred to y for the trader t."

An *allocation*, X, is a set of k commodity bundles, $X(t)$ in R_+^n, such that

$$\sum_{t \in T_k} X(t) \leq \sum_{t \in T_k} I(t).$$

An allocation X is in the *core*, $C(E_k^n)$, if there does not exist any nonempty subset S of T_k and an allocation Y such that

$$\text{(i)}\ Y(t) \succ_t X(t), \qquad \forall t \in S,$$

$$\text{(ii)}\ \sum_{t \in S} Y(t) \leq \sum_{t \in S} I(t).$$

It is well known that for the economy E_2^2 (which is another name for the familiar Edgeworth box) CC' in figure 13 represents the set of allocations in the core.

In the absence of an adequate theory of bargaining one can only specify in broad terms the bargaining costs involved in forming coalitions. As such, we rule out the formation of certain coalitions without delving into the underlying reasons. We shall consider those cores in which no coalition can improve upon their position using their own resources, but these coalitions are restricted by one of the following factors: (1) they are required to be "small" in size; (2) they are required to be "large" in size; or (3) they are required to be "small" in size and made up of members with "similar characteristics." Of course, this is a somewhat crude formalization of the costs of bargaining; for example, under (1), a coalition either faces an infinite cost or, if it is small enough, no cost.

We begin with the discussion of the core where the coalitions are required to have a size smaller than ϵ, ϵ being an arbitrary small number. For convenience we call such cores *ϵc-cores*. Formally, we say that an allocation X is in the *ϵc-core* if there does not exist an allocation y and a coalition S such that

$$\text{(i)}\ Y(t) \succ_t X(t)\ (\forall t \in S),$$

$$\text{(ii)}\ \sum_{t \in S} Y(t) \leq \sum_{t \in S} I(t),$$

(iii) $|S|/|T_k| \leq \epsilon$, where $|S|$ denotes the number of elements in S.

When we compare the above definition with that of the core, the only new factor is (iii), which makes precise the intuitive idea of a coalition being "small" in size.

The ϵc-core depends crucially on ϵ; the smaller the ϵ, the larger the ϵc-core. This is illustrated in figure 13, which depicts the economy E_2^2. Let $\epsilon < \frac{1}{2}$, then all coalitions are inadmissible and the entire Edgeworth box is the ϵc-core. For $\frac{1}{2} \leq \epsilon < 1$, only one-trader coalitions are admissible and the lined area $ICUC'$ is the ϵc-core. For $\epsilon = 1$, all coalitions are allowed to form and the ϵc-core reduces to the core, CC'. If, however, coalitions are required to have a size larger than $1 - \epsilon$, ϵ being an arbitrary small number, then we obtain the *ϵC-cores*. The definition of the ϵC-core requires that we change (iii) in the definition of an ϵc-core and require instead that

$$|S|/|T_k| \geq 1 - \epsilon.$$

Once again it is the relative size of the coalition that is the relevant index. In terms of the Edgeworth box, for $0 \leq \epsilon < \frac{1}{2}$ the ϵC-core is $0_1 0_2$, the set of Pareto-optimal allocations of E_2^2. For $\frac{1}{2} \leq \epsilon \leq 1$, the ϵC-core reduces to the core of E_2^2, namely CC'.

We now consider the final restriction and try to make precise the idea of traders being similar in their characteristics. A trader has only two characteristics, his preferences and his endowment. One can formalize the idea of two agents having similar endowments simply enough. Consider the endowments $I(t)$ and $I(s)$ of traders t and s. Since both $I(t)$ and $I(s)$ are members of R_+^n, one can measure the distance between them (say) by the Euclidean metric. We get the expression

$$\sqrt{\sum_{i=1}^{n} (I_i(t) - I_i(s))^2}.$$

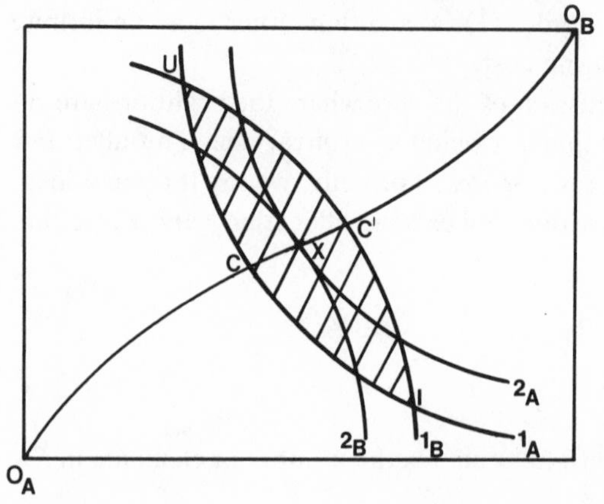

Figure 13. An Edgeworth box and core allocations.

If this is zero, the two agents have the same endowment; if it is not zero but small, the two agents can be said to have similar endowments. The smaller the distance, the more similar the endowments.

The same idea can also be applied to formalize the similarity of the preference orderings $\succ_t$ and $\succ_s$. First, observe that every preference ordering can be represented as a set in $R^n_+ \times R^n_+$, namely the set $\{(x, y) | x \succ_t y; (x, y) \in R^n_+ \times R^n_+\}$. Just as we can measure the distance between two points, we can also measure the distance between two sets (say) by the Hausdorff metric. If this distance is zero, the two agents can be said to have the same preferences; if it is not zero but small, the two agents can be said to have similar preferences. As before, the smaller the distance, the more similar the preferences. Indeed, one can carry out the procedure jointly on the combined space of preferences and endowments by a single metric. We shall then denote this metric by ρ, and $\rho(s, t)$ will measure the similarity of agents with characteristics s and t.

The *ϵϵc-core* is obtained if (iii) in the definition of the ϵc-core is strengthened to read

$$|S|/|T_k| \leq \epsilon;\ S = \bigcup_{i=1}^{\ell} A_i,\ \ell \leq n \text{ where for all } i,$$

$$\rho(s, t) \leq \epsilon.$$

$$s, t \in A_i.$$

Not only is it required that only "small" coalitions form, but it is also stipulated that each coalition can be decomposed into at most as many subcoalitions as there are commodities, with the agents of each subcoalition having similar characteristics. Thus a group of bakers joins up with a group of butchers and so on. We are not saying that all the agents in the parent coalition have similar characteristics. For the economy E^2_2, for any $\epsilon > 0$, we have ϵc-core E^2_2 = ϵϵc-core E^2_2. Since all our restricted cores make it more difficult for a coalition to improve upon any proposed core allocation, it will be true that, for any $\epsilon > 0$ and all n, they all contain the core. Similarly, since the ϵϵc-core restricts coalitions within the ϵc-core, it will always be true that ϵc-core $(E^n_k) \subseteq$ ϵϵc-core (E^n_k).

"Costly" Cores

We now formulate cores with costs of coalition formation; such cores will encompass the ϵc-core and ϵϵc-cores of the previous section. The costs we emphasize are those that depend upon the size of the coalition and the heterogeneity of its members. As a measure of the size of a coalition, we shall use its size relative to the economy, that is, $|S|/|T_k|$, which we denote by $\mathcal{S}(S)$. As argued by Werner Hildenbrand (1972), this is the natural notion in large economies in which we are not interested in individuals per se, but only insofar as these individuals are representative of a group.

The notion of heterogeneity of a coalition to be used will be based upon the important insight of Brigit Grodal (1972). Let $\{A_i\}$ indicate a partition of a coalition S into at most n disjoint subcoalitions. The index of heterogeneity $H(S)$ is then defined as

$$H(S) = \min_{\{A_i\}} \max_{1 \leq i \leq n} \max_{s,\, t \in A_i} \rho(s, t)$$

where $\rho(.\ ,\ .)$ is the metric on preferences and endowments and A_i is a typical member of the partition $\{A_i\}$. $H(S)$ thus measures the maximal amount of heterogeneity within subcoalitions, rather than the maximal distance between members of a coalition. This restriction is necessary because we do not assume that the space of agents' characteristics is compact.

We now postulate that for any coalition S, the costs associated with forming it are given by

$$C(S) = C[H(S), \mathcal{S}(S)].$$

For the rest of the chapter we shall assume the following standing hypothesis:

$$\lim_{x,\, y \to 0} C(x, y) = 0.$$

We can now formulate a core in which explicit account is taken of the resources used in the formation of coalitions, which we shall call an *ℓ-core*. An allocation X is said to be in the *ℓ-core* of E_k^n if there does not exist an allocation Y and a coalition S such that

(i) $Y(t) \succ_t X(t), \qquad t \in S$

(ii) $\sum_{t \in S} Y(t) \leq [\sum_{t \in S} I(t)] - C[H(S), \mathcal{S}(S)].$

Specialization of $C(S)$ to $\epsilon|S|e$ and ϵe leads respectively to the *weak ϵ-core* and the *strong ϵ-core* first discussed by Shapley and Shubik (1966) and Yakar Kannai (1970). By requiring that $C(S) = 0$, for all coalitions such as $|S|/|T_k| \leq \epsilon$, and infinity otherwise, we obtain the ϵc-core of Schmeidler; by requiring in addition that $C(S) = 0$ for all coalitions such that $H(S) \leq \epsilon$, and infinity otherwise, we obtain the $\epsilon\epsilon c$-core of Grodal. The ℓ-core thus generalizes existing notions and satisfies the requirement that costs of coalition formation should vary between coalitions of the same size.

Edgeworth's Conjecture Reformulated

The interesting question that now arises is whether the costly cores introduced can be decentralized, that is, are the costly cores stable against individual actions taken at some suitable set of prices and taxes? Can the proof of Edgeworth's conjecture be extended to cover these more realistic cores? Some positive answers to these questions are given in this section.

Let $E = \{E_k^n\}_{k=1}^{\infty}$ be an unbounded sequence of finite exchange economies that satisfies the following conditions. As n remains fixed, it is omitted in what follows.

(1) There exists $\underline{r} > 0$ such that for all E_k in E,

$$(1/|T_k|) \sum_{t \in T_k} I(t) \geq \underline{r}e.$$

(2) There exists $\bar{r} > 0$ and $m \in N$ such that for all

E_k in E, $|T_k| > m$, for all $\epsilon > 0$,

$$S \subset T_k, \frac{|S|}{|T_k|} \leq \epsilon \text{ implies } (1/|T_k|) \sum_{t \in S} I(t) \leq \bar{r}\,\epsilon\, e.$$

The first condition is a rather routine requirement that every economy that we analyze has enough of every commodity. The second assumption guarantees that in a large enough economy every *numerically negligible* coalition is *economically negligible*. In other words, we are excluding large traders from the large but finite economies that we consider. Finally, we assume that for all economies E_k in E,

(3) The preferences of all traders are *irreflexive*; (no commodity bundle is preferred to itself), and *weakly monotonic*, that is, $x \gg y$ implies $x \succ_t y$. This is a standard assumption. We do not assume transitivity or completeness of preferences.

To motivate the definition of approximate competitive equilibrium it is useful to begin by reformulating the usual definition of a competitive equilibrium. Recall that the pair (p, X), where p is a price system in $R_+^n -$ (0) and X is an allocation, is said to be a *competitive equilibrium* if $L^p(X)$ is empty, where $L^p(X)$ is the set of traders for which one or both the following conditions hold:

(a) $|p \cdot X(t) - p \cdot I(t)| \neq 0$, where $|x|$ denotes the modulus of the number x.

(b) There exists a commodity bundle y in the budget set which is preferred to $X(t)$, (that is, $y \succ_t X(t)$) and $p \cdot y \leq p \cdot I(t)$.

Condition (a) prohibits any trader from spending more than his income; (b) says that no feasible bundle should be preferred to the equilibrium bundle.

We now say that the pair (p, X) is an *ϵ-equilibrium* of E_k if the set of traders $L_\epsilon^p(X)$ is small, that is, $|L_\epsilon^p(X)|/|T_k| \leq \epsilon$. A trader t is in $L_\epsilon^p(X)$ if either of the following conditions holds:

(a) $|p \cdot X(t) - p \cdot I(t)| > \epsilon$,
(b) $\exists y$ such that $p \cdot y \leq p \cdot I(t) - \epsilon$, and $y \succ_t X(t)$, that is, there exists a bundle y in an approximate budget set which is preferred to $X(t)$.

An ϵ-equilibrium is thus a direct generalization of the notion of a competitive equilibrium. We can now state

THEOREM 1. *For any positive number ϵ, however small, all "large enough" finite economies in $\mathcal{E}$ can have their ℓ-cores sustained as ϵ-equilibria.*[2]

To interpret this theorem in economic terms, consider any outcome achieved through bargaining between a group of agents. This bargaining may have an implicit cost in that there are restrictions on the size or characteristics of the coalitions or it may have an explicit cost in terms of the function C. Then the above two results assure us that in either case there exists a system of prices at which almost every trader will keep his core bundle and neither trade it for another nor demand back his initial endowment for further trading. There is one qualification to this statement: every trader has to pay a lump-sum tax of magnitude 2ϵ on his transactions. The position of a typical trader is thus illustrated in figure 14.

The reader may have observed that *almost* has been formalized in terms of relative size. Thus the set of traders for which (a) and (b) do not hold has a size less than ϵ, that is, $|L_\epsilon^p(X)|/|T_k| \leq \epsilon$. As such, ϵ is parametrizing three factors in Theorem 1:

(a) the size of the core;
(b) the magnitude of the lump-sum tax; and
(c) the size of the set of deviants $L_\epsilon^p(X)$.

2. By specializing our theorems to the case where there are no costs of coalition formation, we obtain a generalization of Theorem 3 of Hildenbrand (1974:202), in that our result holds for a sequence of simple economies that need not come from a purely competitive sequence and whose agents' preferences need not be transitive and strictly monotonic. Hildenbrand, however, chose the price p_n from the set of equilibria of a limit economy whereas for our sequence such a limit economy need not exist.

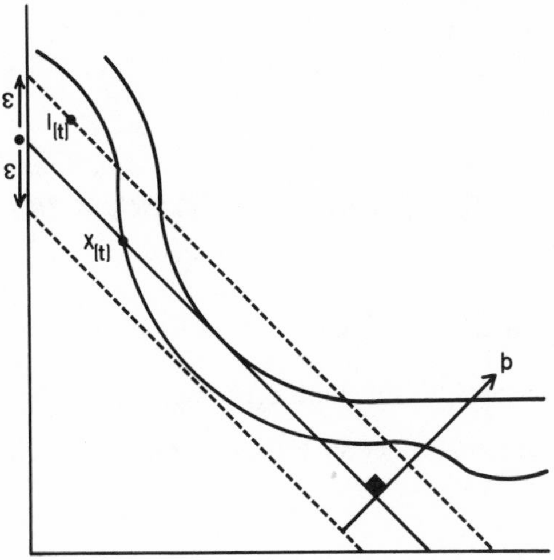

Figure 14. Consumer's optima at ϵ-equilibria.

Proofs

To prove Theorem 1, we formulate a nonstandard exchange economy ξ_ω which captures the behavior of the sequence of large but finite economies E "at infinity." Results that are proved to be true for all ξ_ω can be shown to be approximately true for all "large enough" finite economies by appealing to the proof technique described earlier in the chapter on Pareto-optimality. More specifically, the proof of Theorem 1 proceeds in the following steps. First, we define the nonstandard limit economy ξ_ω and the associated notions of L-core and L-equilibrium. We then show that any allocation in the L-core of ξ_ω can be sustained as an L-equilibrium of ξ_ω. This is the content of Theorem 2. We show next that the ϵc, ϵC, and $\epsilon\epsilon c$-cores of ξ_ω are all contained in the L-core of ξ_ω. This is done by showing that the ℓ-core, which contains the ϵc, ϵC, and $\epsilon\epsilon c$-cores, is itself contained in the L-core. This is accomplished by Lemma 4. Finally, we use both of these steps in conjunction to complete the proof of Theorem 1.

A *nonstandard exchange economy*, ξ_ω, consists of a pair of functions I and P, where $I: T \rightarrow {}^*R^n_+$ and $P: T \rightarrow \mathcal{P}({}^*R^n_+ \times {}^*R^n_+)$ and $\mathcal{P}(A)$ denotes the power set of A.

We shall denote the functions I and P respectively as $(I(t))_{t=1}^{\omega}$ and $(\succ_t)_{t=1}^{\omega}$, where $I(t)$ is to be interpreted as the initial endowment of the tth trader and $\succ_t$ as his preference relation over ${}^*R^n$. We will assume that ξ_ω has the following properties:

(A.1) The function indexing the initial endowments, $I(t)$, is internal.

(A.2) $\frac{|S|}{\omega} \simeq 0 \Rightarrow \frac{1}{\omega} \sum_{t \in S} I(t) \simeq 0.$

(A.3) $\frac{1}{\omega} \sum_{t \in T} I(t) \gg 0.$

(A.4) The relation, Q, where $Q = \{(t, \succ_t) | t \in T, \succ_t \subseteq {}^*R^n_+ \times {}^*R^n_+$ is internal. For all t:

(α) $\succ_t$ is irreflexive.
(β) If $x \gg y$ then $x \succ_t y$.

We shall need the following concepts for this limit economy, ξ_ω.

(D.1) An *allocation* is an internal function Y from T into ${}^*R^n_+$ such that

$$\frac{1}{\omega} \sum_{t \in T} Y(t) = \frac{1}{\omega} \sum_{t \in T} I(t).$$

(D.2) A *coalition* S is an internal subset of T. It is said to be *negligible* if $|S|/\omega \simeq 0$.
(D.3) An allocation Y *blocks* an allocation X if there exists a nonnegligible coalition S such that

(a) $Y(t) \succ_t X(t) \qquad (t \in S)$

(b) $\frac{1}{\omega} \sum_{t \in S} Y(t) \lessapprox \frac{1}{\omega} \sum_{t \in S} I(t).$

(D.4) An allocation Y is in the *L-core* if there exists no allocation that blocks it.
(D.5) A *price system* p is a vector in R^n such that $p > 0$.
(D.6) The tth trader's *budget set*, $B_p(t)$, is $\{x \in {}^*R^n_+ | px \lesssim pI(t)\}$.
(D.7) y is said to be *maximal* in $B_p(t)$ if $y \in B_p(t)$ and $x \succ_t y$ $p \cdot x \gtrsim p \cdot I(t)$.
(D.8) An *L-equilibrium* is defined as a pair (p, X) where p is a price system and X an allocation such that $X(t)$ is maximal for all but a negligible set of traders.

We now turn to showing that the L-core can be sustained as an L-equilibrium. The following lemmas conveniently gather together some earlier results.

LEMMA 1. (i) *For all allocations X, there exists $M \in N$ such that $1/\omega \sum_{t \in T} X(t) \leq Me$.* (ii) *In addition, the set $V' = \{t \in T | X(t)/\omega \neq 0\}$ is contained in an internal set V with $|V|/\omega \simeq 0$.*[3] *(This is Theorem 5.7.)*

3. This important result is from Robert Anderson (1981).

LEMMA 2. *If G is internally bounded,* $1/\omega\ \Sigma_{t\in T}\ G(t)$ *is S-convex. (This is the nonstandard version of Lyapunov's theorem.)*

LEMMA 3. *Let G be an internal correspondence such that* $p \cdot (1/\omega\ \Sigma_{t\in T}\ G(t)) \gtrsim 0$ *and* $0 \in G(t)$ $(\forall t \in T)$. *Then there exists an internal set* $K \subseteq T$, $|K|/\omega \simeq 1$ *such that* $p \cdot x(t) \gtrsim 0$, $(\forall x(t) \in G(t))$ $(\forall t \in K)$. *(Lemma 3 was proved in the course of proving Theorem* 7.1.)

THEOREM 2. *If* ξ_ω *satisfies* A.1–A.4, *then corresponding to any allocation X in the L-core of* ξ_ω, *there exists p such that* (p, X) *is an L-equilibrium of* ξ_ω.[4]

PROOF OF THEOREM 2. X is in the L-core if there does not exist an allocation Y and a nonnegligible subset S such that

$$X(t) \succ_t Y(t) \text{ for all } t \text{ in } S.$$

$$\frac{1}{\omega} \sum_S Y(t) \underset{\not\approx}{\ll} \frac{1}{\omega} \sum_S I(t).$$

(A) We begin by enclosing the core bundles in a suitable internally bounded set. Let X be in the L-core of ξ_ω and let $\ell = \max_T \max_i I_i(t)$. Note that $\ell/\omega \simeq 0$. Pick ℓ' such that $\ell' \in {}^*N - N$ and $\ell'\ell/\omega \simeq 0$. Set $\nu = \ell' d$. Define $F_\nu(t) = \{x(t) \in {}^*R^n \,|\, x(t) \succ X(t) \wedge x(t) \leq \nu e\}$

$$G_\nu(t) = \{F_\nu(t) - I(t)\} \cup \{0\}.$$

$$G_\nu = \frac{1}{\omega} \Sigma\, G_\nu(t).$$

By monotonicity, G_ν is nonempty. By choice of ν, $G_\nu(t)/\omega \simeq 0$ and by Brown's Theorem G_ν is S-convex.

(B) Next, we show that $0 \notin S\text{-int}\ G_\nu$.

Suppose $0 \in S\text{-int}\ G_\nu$.
$\exists h(t) \in G_\nu(t)$ and $1/\omega\ \Sigma\ h(t) \underset{\not\approx}{\ll} 0$.
Let $U = \{t \,|\, h(t) \neq 0\}$.
Because $h(t)/\omega \simeq 0$ for all t, we must have $|U|/\omega \not\simeq 0$.
Define $Z(t) = h(t) + I(t)$ for t in U.
Then $Z(t)$ blocks $X(t)$ via U.

(C) The approximately convex set, G_ν, is now separated by a nonzero hyperplane from the origin.

4. Since even a "small" coalition in an infinite economy contains a very large number of traders, it is an easy modification of the proof to show that the addition of a fixed cost does not alter the result. Any fixed (finite) cost when spread out over the coalition has negligible per capita impact.

$0 \notin S$-int G_ν implies $0 \notin S$-int Q con G_ν, bcause G_ν is S-convex. Or, $bdy(Q\text{-con } G_\nu) \simeq 0$.

By the transfer of the standard separation theorem, $\exists p \neq 0$, such that

$$p \cdot x \gtrsim 0, \qquad \forall x \in Q\text{-con } G_\nu.$$

$$\therefore p \cdot x \gtrsim 0, \qquad \forall x \in G_\nu, \text{ because } G_\nu \text{ is } S\text{-convex.} \tag{1}$$

(D) There exists $G_{\nu''}$ which can be separated by a standard price vector. $p = {}^o p + \tilde{p}$ where $\tilde{p} \simeq 0$. As $\tilde{p} \cdot x \simeq 0$, for all x in any finite cube, $\tilde{p} \cdot x \simeq 0$, for all x in G_ν, for some $\nu' \in {}^*N - N$ by prolongation. ${}^o p \cdot x = p \cdot x - \tilde{p} \cdot x > 0$, $\forall x \in G_{\nu''}$ where $\nu'' = \min\{\nu, \nu'\}$.

(E) We now show that ${}^o p > 0$. Suppose not; that is, ${}^o p_1 \lneqq 0$. Certainly

$$1/\omega\, \Sigma\, (X(t) - I(t)) + (\nu'', 1/\nu'', \ldots, 1/\nu'') \equiv \alpha_{\nu''}$$

is an element of $G_{\nu''}$. But ${}^o p \cdot \alpha_{\nu''} \lesssim 0$, which contradicts (1).

By Lemma 3, we can now show that for all $t \in T''$, $|T''|/\omega \simeq 1$,

$$ {}^o p \cdot x(t) \gtrsim {}^o p \cdot I(t) \text{ for all } x(t) \succ_t X(t),$$

$$x(t) \leq X(t) + I(t) + [1 + \ell(t)]\nu e. \tag{2}$$

Let $J = \{ j \in (1, 2, \ldots, n) | {}^o p_i \gtrsim 0\}$. From above, $J \neq \emptyset$. Let x_J be the restriction of the vector x to components in J. Let e_J be a vector whose J components are unity and all others zero. Without loss of generality assume $\Sigma_{j \in J}\, {}^o p_j = 1$ and use (2) to deduce for all t in T''

$$ {}^o p \cdot x(t) \gtrsim {}^o p \cdot I(t) \text{ for all } x(t) \succ_t X(t);$$

$$x_J(t) \leq X_J(t) + I_J(t) + (1 + \ell(t))\nu e_J. \tag{3}$$

This implies that for all t in T'',

$$p \cdot x(t) \gtrsim p \cdot I(t) \text{ for all } x(t) \succ_t X(t). \tag{4}$$

Suppose not; that is, there exist $\tau \in T''$ and $x(\tau) \succ_t X(\tau)$ such that ${}^o p \cdot x(\tau) \lneqq {}^o p \cdot I(\tau) \leq \ell(\tau)$. Thus $x_J(\tau) \leq \text{Max}_{j \in J}\, (1/{}^o p_i)\ell(\tau)e_I$. Since $(1/{}^o p_i)$ is a standard, we contradict (3).

(F) We finally show that there exists an internal set $K \subseteq T''$, $|K|/\omega \simeq 1$ such that ${}^o p \cdot X(t) \simeq {}^o p \cdot I(t)$ for all t in K.

Given A.4β, (4) implies that ${}^o p \cdot X(t) \gtrsim {}^o p \cdot I(t)$ for all t in T''. If ${}^o p \cdot X(t) \gtrsim {}^o p \cdot I(t)$ for a nonnegligible set of traders, then we contradict the fact that, since X is an allocation, ${}^o p \cdot \Sigma\, X(t) = {}^o p \cdot \Sigma\, I(t)$. Q.E.D.

We now get on the second stage of the argument, namely to show that the cores we are interested in are contained in the L-core. We need

LEMMA 4. *If* ξ_ω *satisfies* A.1–A.4, *then* ℓ*-core* $(\xi_\omega) \subseteq L$*-core* (ξ_ω).

PROOF. Let X be an allocation not in the L-core. Then there exists an allocation Y and a nonnegligible coalition S such that

(i) $Y(t) \succ_t X(t)\ (\forall t \in S)$

(ii) $\frac{1}{\omega} \sum_{t \in S} Y(t) \lneq \frac{1}{\omega} \sum_{t \in S} I(t).$

Now C: $^*R^2 \to {}^*R^n$ is the nonstandard extension of a standard function. Because C is assumed to tend to zero when both of its arguments tend to zero given any $\epsilon \gneq 0$, there exists standard $\eta \gneq 0$, such that

$C(x, y) \leq \epsilon$ for all $|x| \leq \eta$, $|y| \leq \eta$.

Suppose $|S|/\omega \leq \eta$ and $H(S) \leq \eta$. Then certainly

$$\frac{1}{\omega}\{[\sum_{t \in S} Y(t) - I(t)] - C(H(S), \mathbb{S}(S))\}$$

$$= \frac{1}{\omega}\{[\sum_{t \in S} Y(t) - I(t)] - h\} \lneq 0$$

where h is an infinitesimal vector. Thus

$$\sum_{t \in S} Y(t) \leq [\sum_{t \in S} I(t)] - C(H(S), \mathbb{S}(S)),$$

and, for all t in S, $Y(t) \succ X(t)$. So X cannot be in the ℓ-core. Q.E.D.

We are now ready to furnish a proof of Theorem 1.

PROOF OF THEOREM 1. Suppose the theorem is false. Then there exists $\epsilon > 0$ such that $(\forall m \in N)\ (\forall E_k \in E)\ (X_k \in \epsilon$-restricted core $(\xi_k))\ \Lambda$ $\{\exists p \in R^n)|L^p_\epsilon(X_k) > \epsilon\}$. Transfer this sentence to the nonstandard universe and observe that if E satisfies conditions (1) to (3), all nonstandard economies in *E satisfy A.1 to A.4. Note that ϵ-restricted cores of ξ_ω are contained in the L-core of ξ_ω by virtue of Lemma 4. We thus contradict Theorem 1. Q.E.D.

10

Edgeworth's Conjecture with Syndicates or Large Traders

The results that have been established hitherto are all based on the assumption that no one individual forms a significant part of the market; thus all individuals form an infinitesimal part of the market. In reality, however, very few markets can be said to possess the characteristics of a perfectly competitive market. Even agriculture, the textbook example of competition, has increasingly come under the influence of the agribusiness oligopoly. Our attempts to show the relevance of economies with infinite traders led us to investigate the possibility of equivalence between core and competitive equilibria in large but finite economies; similarly, it is incumbent upon us to see whether, and under what conditions, the equivalence theorem holds when some traders are large and significant.

To see how "large" has been modeled in the literature, let us recall that all our results have hitherto been expressed relative to the size, as measured by the number of agents, of the economy. Thus an allocation is approximately feasible if

$$\frac{1}{\omega} \Sigma X(t) \simeq \frac{1}{\omega} \Sigma I(t).$$

This can also be written as

$$\frac{1}{\omega} \Sigma [X(t) - I(t)] \simeq 0 \quad \text{or} \quad \Sigma \frac{1}{\omega} [X(t) - I(t)] \simeq 0.$$

The last expression can be read as saying that the excess demand of each agent is weighted by the infinitesimal $1/\omega$ in order to see its impact upon the aggregate excess demand. One way of introducing large traders in our model is therefore to give such traders a noninfinitesimal weight. For example, with two larger traders, A and B, we can express the aggregate excess demand as

$$\lambda_1(X_A - I_A) + \lambda_2(X_B - I_B) + \frac{1}{\omega} \Sigma [X(t) - I(t)]$$

where λ_1 and λ_2 are both standard positive real numbers, $\lambda_1, \lambda_2 \gtrapprox 0$. Although this method is the one that has been explored most thoroughly in the literature, it must be admitted that, from an economic point of view, it is unsatisfactory. After all, what we really want to know is *why* some individuals come to have weights that are noninfinitesimal and to relate these weights in some way to the economic assets of the large trader. This difficulty was clearly stated by Khan (1976), who called the above definition "unorthodox from the viewpoint of finite economies" and then went on to argue at length:

> A way out of these difficulties is to use the same interpretation as in the idealized case. To quote Shitovitz (1974a), "If X is an allocation, then $X(t)$ is *not* the bundle that is assigned to t but the 'bundle density'. The actual bundle that is assigned to t is, in the case of an oligopolist, $x(t)\mu(t)$". . . . This begs the question as to the actual bundle assigned to t when t is not an oligopolist, since in this case $x(t)\mu(t) = 0$. . . . A way out of these difficulties would be to get rid of the weights altogether and distinguish between large and small traders by the magnitude of their endowments. From the economic point of view this could be more satisfactory since it formulates nonnegligibility of a trader in terms of a factor that is most relevant, his endowment. On the other hand it allows us to get rid of a concept that has no economic underpinnings. (P. 283)

One of the reasons for espousing the use of nonstandard analysis is that it provides a simple way of treating "large" traders in infinite economies by modeling large traders as agents with "infinitely large" endowments. Despite some preliminary results in the dissertation of Khan (1973) this is a largely unexplored field and it is to be hoped that future work will bring to light the utility of nonstandard analysis for these problems.[1]

A different interpretation of a larger trader is to view each such trader as the consolidation of a large number of small traders, whom it may therefore be more appropriate to call a "syndicate." We may think of a group of ν traders in an economy with ω agents, where $\nu/\omega \gtrapprox 0$, where all ν traders have identical endowments and preferences. This group may perceive that

1. The little success that has been obtained so far requires the imposition of homothetic preferences upon the large trader. This is hardly satisfactory. If any progress is to be made along the lines of treating monopolists as those agents who hold significant amounts of endowments, some way must be found to circumvent the issues posed by the insightful counterexamples of Aumann (1975). Through a series of examples Aumann shows that there is no necessary relationship between having monopoly power, either in measure-theoretic or commodity terms, and obtaining a most-favored allocation.

it would be to their advantage to act as a unified block vis-à-vis the rest of the economy, and they are then perceived by the small traders as a "large" trader.[2] Under this interpretation, giving the syndicate a noninfinitesimal weight in the aggregate excess demand simply indicates that it represents ν identical traders (with $\nu/\omega \gnapprox 0$). If we take this approach, however, we have left the question of monopolists and oligopolists wide open.

Statement of Model and Theorems

Let $T \subseteq {}^*N$ be a set $(1, 2, \ldots, \omega)$ where $\omega \in {}^*N - N$. Let $T_1 \subseteq T$ be the set $(1, 2, \ldots, m)$ where m is a standard natural number. Let $T_0 = T - T_1$. T is to be interpreted as the set of traders, a finite subset T_1 of whom are large in the sense to be specified below. We can now define:

D.1. *A nonstandard exchange economy*, ξ, consists of a triple of functions I, P, and λ where $I: T \to {}^*R^n_+$, $P: T \to \mathcal{P}({}^*R^n_+ \times {}^*R^n_+)$ and $\lambda: T \to {}^*R$.

We shall denote these functions respectively as $I(t)$, $\succ_t$, and $\lambda(t)$ where for all t in T, $I(t)$ is the tth traders endowment, $\succ_t$ his preference relation, and $\lambda(t)$ his weight in the economy. We shall assume that $\lambda(t) = 1/\omega$ for all t in T_0, and $\lambda(t)$ is a real number for t in T_1. The model accepts the $\lambda(t)$, for t in T_1, as exogenous and has nothing to say about how they are determined. We will assume that ξ satisfies the following properties:

A.1. The function I indexing the initial endowment is internal.
A.2. $\Sigma_{t \in T} I(t)\lambda(t) \lesssim \bar{r}$ where $\bar{r}$ is a standard vector.
A.3. The relation Q, where $Q = \{(t, \succ_t) \mid t \in T, \succ_t \subseteq {}^*R^n_+ \times {}^*R^n_+\}$, is internal for all t in T. In addition,

(α) $\succ_t$ is irreflexive, transitive, monotonic, and continuous for all t in T.
(β) $\succ_t$ is convex and complete for all t in T_1.

A.4. $\lambda(t)$ is a positive infinitesimal for all t in T_0 and is a standard positive number for all t in T_1.

It is in the sense of A.4. that T_1 is the set of large traders. We shall need the following concepts for our limit economy:

D.2. An *assignment* is an internal function from T into ${}^*R^n_+$.
D.3. An *allocation* is an assignment Y such that

$$\sum_{t \in T} Y(t)\lambda(t) = \sum_{t \in T} I(t)\lambda(t).$$

2. See Gabszewicz and Dreze (1971).

D.4. A *coalition* S is an internal subset of T. S is said to be *nonnegligible* if $\lambda(S) = \Sigma_{t \in S} \lambda(t) \gtrsim\!\!\!\!\!/\ 0$.

It is important to note this definition of negligibility. A coalition S may be "numerically negligible" (that is, $|S|/|T| \simeq 0$), or "economically negligible" (that is, $\Sigma_{t \in S} I(t)\lambda(t) \simeq 0$ if $I(t) \simeq 0$ for all t in S), without being negligible in the sense of D.4. This situation parallels that for a measure-theoretic economy with atoms.

D.5. An allocation Y *blocks* an allocation X if there exists a nonnegligible coalition S such that

(a) $Y(t) \succ_t X(t)$ $(\forall t \in S)$,
(b) $\Sigma_{t \in S} Y(t)\lambda(t) \lesssim \Sigma_{t \in S} I(t)\lambda(t)$.

D.6. An allocation X is in the *core* if there exists no allocation that blocks it.

D.7. A *price system* p, is a standard vector in $^*R^n$ such that $p > 0$.

D.8. The tth trader's *budget set*, $B_p(t)$, is $\{x \in {}^*R^n_+ | p \cdot x \lesssim p \cdot I(t)\}$.

D.9. $X(t)$ is *maximal* in $B_p(t)$ if $X(t) \in B_p(t)$ and $y \succ_t X(t)$ implies $p \cdot y \gtrsim p \cdot I(t)$.

D.10. A *competitive equilibrium* is defined as a pair (p, X) where p is a price system and X an allocation such that $X(t)$ is maximal for almost all t in T.

Note that the set K is almost equal to the set T if $T - K$ is a negligible set.

We are now ready to state our theorems.

THEOREM 1. *If ξ satisfies* A.1.–A.4., *then corresponding to any allocation X in the core, there exists a price system p such that*

(a) $y \succ_t X(t), \Rightarrow p \cdot y \gtrsim p \cdot X(t)$ *for almost all t in T,*
(b) $p \cdot X(t) \lesssim p \cdot I(t)$ *for almost all t in T_0.*

Two traders are said to be of the same *type* if they have the same preferences and the same endowment. They are said to be of the same *kind* if they also have the same weight.

THEOREM 2. *Let there be at least two traders in T_1 all of the same type. Then, under the assumptions of Theorem* 1, *corresponding to any allocation X in the core, there exists a price system p such that (p, X) is a competitive equilibrium.*

THEOREM 3. *Let $T_1 = \cup_{i=1}^d A_i$ such that each A_i contains $m \geq 2$ atoms of the same kind. Then, under the assumptions of Theorem* 1, *cor-*

responding to any allocation in the core, there exists a price system such that

(a) $y \succ_t X(t), \Rightarrow p \cdot y \gtrsim p \cdot X(t)$ *for almost all t in T,*
(b) $p \cdot X(t) \simeq p \cdot I(t)$ *for almost all t in* T_0,
(c) $p \cdot X(t) \simeq p \cdot X(s)$ *for all* $s, t \in A_i$, *for all i.*

Let w be any large trader or atom in ξ. The *split atom*, W, is a star-finite set such that all t in W are of the same type as w and

$$\lambda(w) \simeq \sum_{t \in W} \lambda(t).$$

The economy obtained after splitting some of the large traders in all but one of the A_i will be denoted by $\bar{\xi}$.

THEOREM 4. *Let* ξ *and* $\bar{\xi}$ *satisfy the assumptions of Theorem 3. Then, corresponding to any standardly bounded allocation X in the core of* $\bar{\xi}$, *there exists a price system p such that* (p, X) *is a competitive equilibrium.*

The interpretation of Theorem 1 is quite straightforward. An allocation X in the core must, of course, be Pareto-optimal and will therefore have a system of efficiency prices p associated with it. If $p \cdot X(t) = p \cdot I(t)$ for all traders, this allocation is also competitive. In general, however, we cannot expect all core allocations to be competitive, so that some traders will have $p \cdot X(t) > p \cdot I(t)$ and others will have $p \cdot X(t) < p \cdot I(t)$. Theorem 1 says that only $p \cdot X(t) > p \cdot I(t)$ can hold for the larger trader and $p \cdot X(t) < p \cdot I(t)$ for the small traders; that is, monetarily, the large trader can only gain and the small trader only lose. In this sense, then, the advantage of being a large trader can be precisely stated.

The content of Theorem 2 is more surprising. It says that if under the conditions of Theorem 1, we introduce a second large trader, the advantage possessed by the large traders completely disappears. Every core allocation can now be shown to be perfectly competitive, and we have regained the full force of Edgeworth's conjecture. Nonetheless, despite its simplicity, Theorem 2 leaves us a little uneasy, as Shitovitz (1974a) expressed very clearly:

> For definiteness think of a town with a single large hotel. We have seen . . . that the monopolist can exploit the small traders. . . . The result is intuitively reasonable. . . . Suppose now a small entrepreneur enters the scene with a small Hotel or Pension. If the Pension is very small, one feels that the situation should not change very much. But this is false; no matter how small the additional oligopolist is, the large hotel has suddenly lost all its power and must take competitive prices as if the town was full of all kinds of hotels. One feels that intuitively the original monopolist has not, in fact, lost his power. The large hotel can, and probably will simply ignore the new entrepreneur. (P. 472)

Theorems 3 and 4 are extensions of Theorem 2 to cases in which we have more than one type of large trader. In Theorem 3 we have finitely many kinds of large traders with at least two large traders of each kind. We can now show that the small traders are not monetarily exploited, but we cannot rule out the possibility that *some* of the large traders are monetarily exploited. Theorem 4 focuses on a situation which is very much like that in Theorem 3 except that we now consider the consequences when some of the large traders are split up. That the equivalence of Theorem 2 can be regained without having to split up all the large traders has been interpreted by Shitovitz as indicating that oligopolistic markets may be turned competitive by trust-busting only some of the monopolists.[3]

Proofs of Results

We can now furnish the proofs of Theorems 1–4. The argument follows that set out in earlier chapters and differs in form (though not in substance) from those of Shitovitz (1974a) or Khan (1976).

LEMMA 1. *Let X be an allocation. Then under* A.2. *and* A.4. *the set* $[t \in T_0 | X(t)\lambda(t) \neq 0 \text{ or } I(t)\lambda(t) \neq 0]$ *is contained in an internal set V such that* $\lambda(V) \simeq 0$.

PROOF. The proof follows directly from that of Theorem 5.7. Henceforth we will simply ignore this negligible set V.

PROOF OF THEOREM 1. Let X be an allocation in the core. Define the following sets:

$$F(t) = \{x(t) \in {}^*R^n_+ | x(t) \succ_t X(t)\}$$

$$G(t) = \{F(t) - I(t)\} \cup \{0\} \text{ for } t \text{ in } T_0$$

$$= \{F(t) - I(t)\} \text{ for } t \text{ in } T_1.$$

By Brown's theorem

$$\sum_{T_0} G(t)\lambda(t)$$

is S-convex. Since the large traders have convex preferences,

$$\sum_{T_1} G(t)\lambda(t)$$

3. Asymptotic results for somewhat weaker versions of Theorems 1, 2, 3, and 4 may be found in Khan (1976). Subsequently, measure-theoretic methods were used to obtain asymptotic results by Trockel (1976). An earlier attempt by Gabszewicz (1977) used a specific example involving homothetic preferences.

is, of course, convex. Hence

$$G = \sum_T G(t)\lambda(t)$$

is S-convex.

I. We now show that $0 \notin G$. If not, there exists an internal function $h(t) \in G(t)$ such that $\Sigma_T h(t) = 0$. Let $S' = \{t \in T | h(t) = 0\}$, then S' and $S = T - S'$ are both internal. Define $Y(t) = h(t) + I(t)$ for $t \in S$. Then $Y(t) \succ X(t)$ and $\Sigma Y(t) = \Sigma h(t) + \Sigma I(t) = \Sigma I(t)$. So the coalition S blocks X via $Y(t)$, $t \in S$. This contradicts X being in the core.

II. By the same separation argument used in chapter 6, there exists a standard vector $p \neq 0$ such that $p \cdot x \gtrsim 0$ for all $x \in G$.

III. We now show that, for almost all t in T, $p \cdot x(t) \gtrsim 0$ for all x in $G(t)$. Suppose not; then there exists a nonnegligible subset S, such that $\lambda(S) \gtrapprox 0$ and $z(t) \in G(t)$ for all $t \in S$ with $p \cdot z(t) \lessapprox 0$.

$$\begin{aligned} \text{Set } h(t) &= 0 \text{ for } t \text{ in } T - S \\ &= z(t) \text{ for } t \text{ in } S. \end{aligned}$$

Then $h(t)$ is an internal selection from $G(t)$, but if $y = \Sigma_T h(t)\lambda(t)$, then $p \cdot y < 0$, contradicting result II. The fact that $p \gtrapprox 0$ follows exactly as in chapter 6 and the proof will not be repeated.

IV. To see that $p \cdot X(t) \leq p \cdot I(t)$ for all t in T_0, define $e(t) = X(t) - I(t)$ and note that

$$\sum_{T_0} e(t)\lambda(t) + \sum_{T_1} e(t)\lambda(t) = 0.$$

Denote $\Sigma_{T_1} f(t)\lambda(t)$ by $f(\alpha)$, where $f(t)$ is a selection from $F(t)$, that is, $f(t) \in F(t)$, $t \in T_1$.

Let $S = \{t \in T_0 | p \cdot X(t) \gtrapprox p \cdot I(t)\}$ and suppose $\lambda(S) \gtrapprox 0$.
Then $p \cdot e(\alpha) + \Sigma_S\, p \cdot e(t) + \Sigma_{T_0 - S}\, p \cdot e(t) = 0$.
Hence, $|p \cdot e(\alpha)| \lessapprox |\Sigma_S\, p \cdot e(t)|$.
Now define a selection $h(t)$ as follows:

$$\begin{aligned} h(t) &= e(t), \qquad t \in S \\ &= e(t), \qquad t \in T_1 \\ &= 0, \qquad t \in T_0 - S. \end{aligned}$$

$h(t)$ is an internal selection from G. But $p \cdot h(t) = p \cdot e(\alpha) + \Sigma_S\, p \cdot e(t) \lessapprox 0$, contradicting II. Hence $p \cdot X(t) \lesssim p \cdot I(t)$ for almost all t in T_0.

Q.E.D.

The method of proof employed for Theorems 2, 3, and 4 differs from, but is equivalent to, the methods used by Shitovitz and by Khan, and a few words need to be said on the relationship between the two proof techniques. If $G(t)$ referred to the set of points preferred to a core allocation, then we have hitherto been considering $G = \Sigma_T [G(t) \cup \{0\}]$. This method enables us to consider any coalition S we like by simply choosing $\{0\}$ for the members of $T - S$. When some of the members of T are atoms, however, then $G(t) \cup \{0\}$ is *not* a convex set for these atoms, and, since they are atoms, we cannot make this nonconvexity negligible by aggregation. To continue to use our earlier method we would therefore have to consider several sets; in the case when there are two large traders, agents α and β for example, we need to look at three sets,

$$G_\alpha = G(\alpha) \cup \sum_{T_0} [G(t) \cup \{0\}] \cdot \lambda(t)$$

$$G_\beta = G(\beta) \cup \sum_{T_0} [G(t) \cup \{0\}] \cdot \lambda(t)$$

$$G = G(\alpha) \cup G(\beta) \cup \sum_{T_0} [G(t) \cup \{0\}] \cdot \lambda(t).$$

For convenience, define

$$G' = \sum_{T_0} [G(t) \cup \{0\}] \cdot \lambda(t).$$

Our problem is to find a separating hyperplane for $G \cup G_\alpha \cup G_\beta$ or, equivalently, for $\mathrm{co}(G' \cup G_\alpha \cup G_\beta)$ where co denotes "convex hull." To make the intuitive argument of the next paragraphs more readable, references to infinitesimals are omitted.

Hitherto we have associated certain "convex" sets with each core allocation, separated the "convex" set from the origin, and shown that we have an efficiency equilibrium; that is, using the separating hyperplane as prices, p, "all" individuals are maximizing their preferences subject to a budget limited by $p \cdot X(t)$. This is not a competitive equilibrium because all we know is that $p \cdot X(t) \leq p \cdot I(t)$, rather than $p \cdot X(t) = p \cdot I(t)$.

We now wish to establish that, under the hypothesis of Theorem 2, $p \cdot X(t) = p \cdot I(t)$. This may be written as two inequalities (a) $p \cdot X(t) \leq p \cdot I(t)$ and (b) $p \cdot X(t) \geq p \cdot I(t)$. Since the vector $e(t) = X(t) - I(t)$ already belongs to $G(t)$, if we are to obtain both (a) and (b), it is necessary to establish that the vector $-e(t) = I(t) - X(t)$ can be consistently introduced into the sets we wish to separate. With a monopolist this amendment is clearly not feasible in general for the following reason:

$$e(\alpha) + e(t_1) + e(t_2) = 0 \text{ (feasibility)}$$

where it suffices to assume that there are only three traders: the monopolist, α, and two traders, t_1 and t_2 (t_1 and t_2 may be considered as aggregates of small traders if so desired). Hence,

$$p \cdot e(\alpha) + p \cdot e(t_1) + p \cdot e(t_2) = 0$$

and $p \cdot f(\alpha) + p \cdot f(t_1) + p \cdot f(t_2) \geq 0$ for any selection $f(\alpha), f(t_1), f(t_2)$ from $G(\alpha)$, $G(t_1)$ and $G(t_2)$.

If $-e(t_1)$ is an admissible selection from $G(t_1)$, then consider

$$\begin{aligned} p \cdot e(\alpha) - p \cdot e(t_1) + p \cdot e(t_2) \\ &= p \cdot e(\alpha) + p \cdot e(t) + p \cdot e(t_2) - 2p \cdot e(t_1) \\ &= -2p \cdot e(t_1) < 0, \text{ a contradiction.} \end{aligned}$$

It is helpful to see the situation in a diagram. In figure 15, G' and $G(\alpha)$ are shown separately. Figure 16 shows $H_\alpha = G(\alpha) + G'$. Note that the hyperplane that separates H_α at 0 need not pass through $e(\alpha)$. In fact, $e(\alpha)$ will generally lie above this hyperplane. This illustrates the case of a monopoly market. With two large traders, however, the situation changes drastically. A feasible allocation is given by

$$e(\alpha) + e(\beta) + \sum_{T_0} e(t) = 0.$$

Suppose our hypotheses also imply that $e(\alpha) = \mu e(\beta)$, with $0 < \mu < 1$. Then an allocation is given by

$$(1 + \mu)e(\alpha) + \sum_{T_0} e(t) = 0.$$

Figures 17 and 18 are the corresponding diagrams when we have two large traders. If we now define

$$H'_{\alpha\beta} = G(\alpha) + G(\beta) + G'$$

then it can be seen that $H'_{\alpha\beta}$ contains both $e(\alpha) + e(\beta)$ and $-[e(\alpha) + e(\beta)]$; that is, $e(\alpha)$ and $-e(\alpha)$ are both on the boundary of $H'_{\alpha\beta}$. Geometrically, it is now obvious that any separating hyperplane through the origin must pass through $e(\alpha)$ and $-e(\alpha)$. Hence we must have $p \cdot e(\alpha) = 0$. It follows that $p \cdot e(\beta) = 0$, and it will follow that $p \cdot e(t) = 0$ for t in T_0.

Since $H'_{\alpha\beta}$ contains both $e(\beta)$ and $-e(\beta)$, the separating hyperplane given by p must contain the entire line through these two points. It is now geometrically plausible that when we take selections involving $-e(t)$ for any subset of traders, the sum is still in co $H'_{\alpha\beta}$. Let us check the case when we choose $-e(t)$ for all traders in T_0. The sum $e(\alpha) + e(\beta) + \Sigma -e(t) = [e(\alpha) + e(\beta)] = \delta$ (say), $[\Sigma\, e(t) = e(\alpha) + e(\beta)]$. Since $e(\alpha) + e(\beta) = (1 + \mu)e(\alpha)$ and the separating hyperplane goes through both $e(\alpha)$ and $e(\beta)$, we see that δ also lies on the hyperplane that contains $e(\alpha)$, $e(\beta)$ and $-e(\beta)$. This suggests that we can consistently augment each $G(t)$ by $-e(t)$.

Having motivated the definition of the sets we shall use, it is relatively simple to prove Theorem 2.

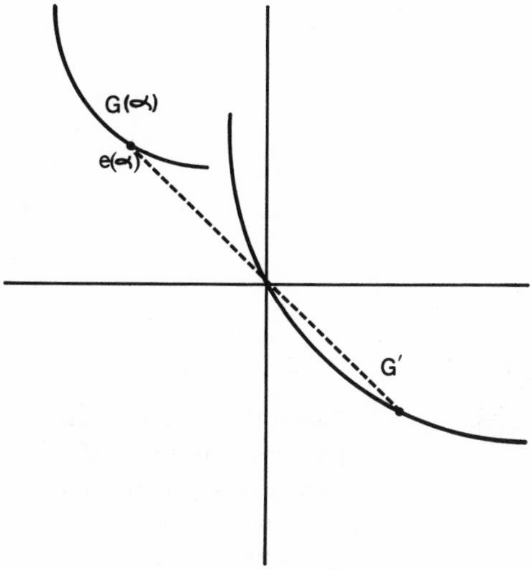

Figure 15. The preferred-to sets for an atom α and the aggregate of small traders.

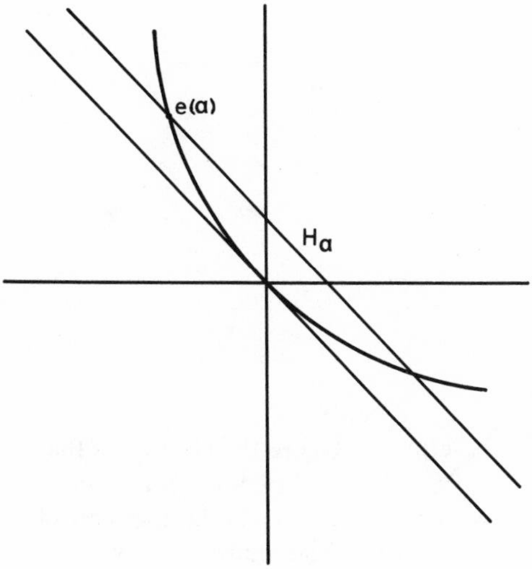

Figure 16. The sum of the preferred-to sets of the atom and the aggregate of small traders.

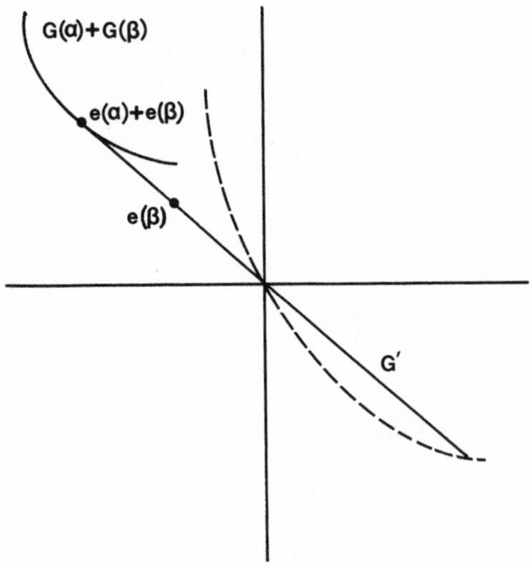

Figure 17. The preferred-to sets for the aggregate of small traders and the sum of the preferred-to sets with two atoms, α and β.

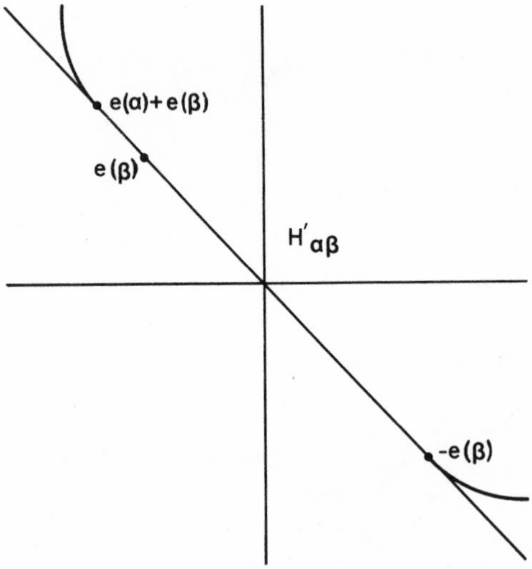

Figure 18. The sum of the preferred-to sets for two atoms and the aggregate of small traders.

PROOF OF THEOREM 2. Define the sets $H(t)$ as follows:

$$H(t) = G(t) \cup \{I(t) - X(t)\} \qquad \text{for } t \text{ in } T_0.$$
$$= G(t) \qquad \text{for } t \text{ in } T_1.$$

The proof that $G_H = \Sigma\, H(t)\lambda(t)$ is S-convex follows exactly as before since Brown's theorem requires only that the vectors being summed are infinitesimal and does not care how they arise. The proof of $0 \notin G_H$ is unchanged. The existence of a separating hyperplane $p \neq 0$, which gives $p \cdot h(t) \geq 0$, $h(t) \in H(t)$, for almost all t in T_0. If we now select $h(t) = I(t) - X(t)$, we get $p \cdot I(t) \geq p \cdot X(t)$. This concludes the proof.

A close examination of the intuition leading to the proof of Theorem 2 shows that the argument will be valid whenever the following standing hypothesis is met: "There is a standard μ, with $0 < \mu < 1$ such that for each k, $k \geq 1$, i.e., for each type of atomic trader, there is a coalition $B_k \subseteq T_k'$ with $\lambda(B_k) = \mu\lambda(T_k')$. The collection $\{T_j'\}$ is a partition of T_1 into equivalence classes of large traders of the same type" (Khan, 1976:291). The hypotheses of Theorems 3 and 4 are simply different ways of ensuring that the standing hypothesis stated above is met. It is left as an exercise for the reader to show that the proofs of these theorems follow from the above remarks and hints.[4]

4. The equivalence of the core and competitive allocations has also been shown by Gabszewicz and Mertens (1971) with the help of a condition on the relative proportions of large and small traders of given types. The condition itself is not at all intuitive, and an economic interpretation of the condition has been obtained only by imposing the strong condition of homogeneous preferences on all traders. In a very real sense therefore the interpretation of Gabszewicz and Mertens's "extravagant condition" still remains open. The nonstandard proof of Gabszewicz and Mertens's result is nonetheless illuminating. The principal complication in their original proof lies in showing that all traders of the same type receive identical utilities in the core. Equal treatment is directly obtained by nonstandard methods, however, and, in an unpublished paper, Khan (1977b) has provided a nonstandard proof of Gabszewicz and Mertens's results.

IV

RELATIONSHIP WITH STANDARD METHODS

11

Turning Nonstandard Proofs into Finite Proofs: Anderson's Theorem

Those who have followed the literature on large economies will probably have been struck that some of the latest, and apparently most general, results on the core equivalence theorem and the existence of approximate equilibria use neither measure theory nor nonstandard analysis. The most famous such result is a theorem of Robert Anderson (1978), which provides a general core equivalence theorem for finite economies. This short chapter will therefore focus on how nonstandard proofs lead to finite proofs by a closer study of Anderson's equivalence theorem. The careful reader will then see how Khan and Rashid (1982) was translated to Anderson, Khan, and Rashid (1982).

Suppose, then, that we have a nonstandard proof of the core equivalence theorem. A proof is nothing but a string of symbols that we can interpret, written down in a prescribed manner. Each line of the proof has to follow from the previous one either by one of the accepted rules of logic or because of one of the axioms we have adopted. If someone came by and looked at the entire proof (assume we have prefixed the rules of logic and our axioms at the head of the proof), how would he know if the proof was about R or $^*R$? If the proof had a line that read

$$\delta \text{ is an infinitesimal, i.e., } \delta \simeq 0, \tag{1}$$

we would immediately realize that we are in $^*R$ since infinitesimals do not exist in R. If, however, the sentence read

$$(\forall \delta \in R_+)(\exists n \in N)(|S_n - S| < \delta), \tag{2}$$

then we have no way of telling from the sentence itself whether we are talking about a convergent sequence in the reals or in the nonstandard reals.

The difference between (1) and (2) is that (1) contains an external concept, infinitesimals, but (2) does not; (2) is an internal statement. As such, looked at in isolation, (2) is just as much a standard sentence as a nonstandard one. If an entire proof can be written down in purely internal fashion—without any reference to external entities—this proof is also a finite proof. The trick in converting nonstandard proofs into finite proofs lies in being able to rewrite each external statement in an equivalent internal fashion. Let us now examine the core equivalence theorem from this point of view.

If X is a core allocation and $X(t)$ is the bundle obtained by trader t, let $P(t)$ denote the set of all points preferred by t to $X(t)$ and let $G(t) \equiv P(t) - I(t)$, that is, the set of all *net* preferred bundles. The core equivalence theorem essentially relies on three steps:

1. $0 \notin \Sigma\, G(t)$.
2. $\Sigma\, G(t)$ is (approximately) convex.
3. Separating $\Sigma\, G(t)$ from 0 by an appropriate hyperplane.

The challenge is to establish each step by an internal proof.

Our earlier definition of a core allocation was that it could not be blocked by any nonnegligible coalition. Because "nonnegligible" is not an internal notion, it will have to be replaced by the internal condition "nonempty." It is an easy exercise to see that exactly the same argument as before is valid for step 1 with the new definition.

Establishing the approximate convexity of $\Sigma\, G(t)$ is a little more subtle. The earliest proofs of this fact used Loeb's theorem, in which infinitesimal convexity of a vector measure is proved. If we have no further information on the infinitesimal approximation, there is no way to avoid the external notion of infinitesimal in our proof. Suppose, however, we can find an explicit formula for the extent of the infinitesimal error. Instead of saying,

$$\Sigma\, G(t) = \text{convex set} + \text{infinitesimal},$$

we can now say,

$$\Sigma\, G(t) = \text{convex set} + g(n), \tag{3}$$

where $g(n)$ is an explicit formula, giving us the error for any integer n; the fact that $g(n)$ is an infinitesimal when $n \in {}^*N - N$ follows from the formula and no longer has to be directly stated. Because (3) is an internal statement, it can also be considered a finite statement. For any finite economy with n traders, (3) will tell us the divergence of $\Sigma\, G(t)$ from a convex set. This divergence will be finite in all finite economies, but it will decrease as the economy gets larger, becoming infinitesimal for $n \in {}^*N - N$.

If we rewrite (3) as

$$\text{Convex set} = \Sigma\, G(t) - g(n),$$

we can separate the origin from the convex set and thus approximately separate the origin from $\Sigma\, G(t)$. The error made in this approximation is then distributed either to traders, budget sets, or aggregate feasibility as before.

The only remaining question therefore is whether we can successfully find an explicit $g(n)$ that will enable us to conduct the proof in internal fashion. Loeb's original proof was concerned only with showing the error to be infinitesimal and so made no effort to keep exact track of the size of the infinitesimal. Nonetheless, since Loeb based his theorem on a result of Ernest Steinitz in which explicit bounds can be found, there is no doubt that Loeb's proof could be easily modified to provide the explicit $g(n)$. A simpler approach is to use the Shapley-Folkman theorem, which was tailor-made for the problem at hand and tells directly the maximal number of individuals who will not be in the "convex part" of $G(t)$. Since this number is just the dimension of commodity space, N, so long as we work with economies with a fixed number of commodities, the aggregate discrepancy from an exact convex set can only be the nonmaximal bundles of N agents. Under reasonable assumptions this quantity remains fixed or grows slowly relative to the number of agents. As a result, the per capita discrepancy goes to zero, and we have a proof of the core equivalence theorem. Anderson's original proof is repeated below, with an indication of how each step relates to the above exposition. Because we will be working throughout in a finite-dimensional space, it will be useful to recall both definitions and notation.

Suppose $x \in R^n$, $y \in R^n$ and $A \subset R^n$, $B \subseteq R^n$. x_i denotes the ith component of x:

$$\|x\|_\infty = \max_{1 \le i \le n} |x_i|, \qquad \|x\|_1 = \sum_{i=1}^{n} |x_i|$$

$$e = (1, \ldots, 1) \in R^n$$

$$x \le y \quad \text{if} \quad x_i \le y_i \quad \text{for} \quad 1 \le i \le n$$

$$x \ll y \quad \text{if} \quad x_i < y_i \quad \text{for} \quad 1 \le i \le n$$

$$A + B = \{x + y : x \in A, y \in B\}$$

con A is the convex hull of A

$$R^n_+ = \{x \in R^n : x \ge 0\}.$$

Let P denote the set of preferences (binary relations on R^n_+), which satisfy

(i) weak monotonicity: $x \gg \; \Rightarrow x \succ y$
(ii) free disposal: $x \gg y, y \succ z \Rightarrow x \succ z$

where x $\}$ y means $(x, y) \in \{$ for $\} \in P$. Note that (ii) is weaker than transitivity, and no continuity is assumed.

Definition: An *exchange economy* is a map $\xi : T \to P \times R^n_+$, where T is a finite set, to be interpreted as the set of traders. For $t \in T$, let $\}_t$ be the projection of $\xi(t)$ onto P and $I(t)$ the projection of $\xi(t)$ onto R^n_+. $\}_t$ is interpreted as the preference of t and $I(t)$ as his endowment. An *allocation* is a map $X : T \to R^n_+$ such that $\Sigma_T X(t) = \Sigma_T I(t)$.

A *coalition* is a nonempty subset of T. An allocation X is *blocked* by a coalition S if there exist $y : S \to R^n_+$ with $\Sigma_S y(t) = \Sigma_S I(t)$ such that $y(t) \} X(t)$ for all $t \in S$. The *core* of ξ, $C(\xi)$, is the set of all allocations that are not blocked by any coalition. A *price vector* p is a vector in R^n_+ such that $\|p\|_1 = 1$. Let $\mathcal{L}$ denote the set of all prices.

THEOREM (ANDERSON). *Let $\xi : T \to P \times R^n_+$ be a finite exchange economy with $|T| = R$. Let $M = \sup\{\|I(t_1) + \cdots + I(t_n)\|_\infty : t_1, \ldots, t_n \in T\}$. If $X \in C(\xi)$, there exists $p \in \mathcal{L}$ such that*

(i) $\dfrac{1}{k} \Sigma_T |p \cdot (X(t) - I(t))| < \dfrac{2M}{k}$

(ii) $\dfrac{1}{k} \Sigma_T |\inf\{p \cdot (x - I(t)) : x \}_t X(t)\}| < \dfrac{2M}{k}.$

PROOF. Define $G(t) = \{y - I(t) : y \}_t X(t)\} \cup \{0\}$ and

$$G = \frac{1}{m} \Sigma_T G(t).$$

Step 1 consists of showing that 0 is not interior to G. The proof is by contradiction.

If 0 is interior to G, then there exists $y \in G$, $y \ll 0$; that is, there exists $y(t) \in G(t)$ such that $y = 1/n \Sigma y(t)$. Let

$$V = \{t \in T : y(t) \neq 0\} \quad \text{and} \quad z(t) = y(t) + I(t) - \frac{m}{|V|} y$$

for t in V. Then $z(t) \gg y(t) + I(t)$ and $z(t) \}_t X(t)$, for all $t \in V$. By property (ii) of preferences,

$$\Sigma_V z(t) = \Sigma_V \left[y(t) + I(t) - \frac{m}{|V|} y \right] = \Sigma_V y(t) + \Sigma_V I(t) - my$$

$$= my + \Sigma_V I(t) - my = \Sigma_V I(t).$$

Hence V blocks X, so $X \notin C(\xi)$, a contradiction.

In Step 2 we try to show that G differs from a convex set by a determinate (and, we hope, very small) amount.

Let $g = (M/m) \cdot e$. Suppose $x \in (\text{con } G) \cap \{w \in R^n : w \ll -g\}$. By the Shapley-Folkman theorem we can write

$$x = \frac{1}{m} [\sum_{B_1} y(t) + \sum_{B_2} y'(t)]$$

where B_1 and B_2 form a partition of T and B_2 contains at most n agents. The important point about this decomposition of x is that all the $y(t)$ lie in con $G(t)$, and all those in B_1 lie in $G(t)$ as well. As a result, it is reasonable to interpret $\Sigma_{B_2} y(t)$ as indicating the extent to which G is not convex. To get a measure of the nonconvexity, we proceed as follows:

Let $\{t_1, \ldots, t_p\}$ denote the elements of B_2 with $p \leq n$. Let $y'(t) = 0$ if $t = t_i, i = 1, \ldots, p$ and let $y'(t) = y(t)$ otherwise. Since $G(t_i) \geq -I(t_i)$, con $G(t_i) \geq -I(t_i)$. Let

$$h = \frac{1}{n} \sum_T g'(t).$$

Then $h \in G$, and

$$h = x - \frac{1}{n} \sum_{i=1}^{p} g(t_i) \leq x + \frac{1}{n} \sum_{i=1}^{p} I(t_i) \leq x + z \ll 0.$$

But $h \in G$, so h cannot be $\ll 0$, and our assumption that $\{\text{con } G\} \cap \{w \in R^n : w \ll -g\}$ is nonempty is false. So these two convex sets are disjoint. Hence G does not contain 0 in its interior and con G does not contain $-g$ in its interior. This serves to provide a bound between the convex set, con G, and the set we are interested in, G.

Step 3 applies the separating hyperplane theorem to the disjoint, convex sets con G and $\{w \in R^n : w \ll -g\}$ and shows that the hyperplane provides us with the appropriate system of prices. By the separating hyperplane theorem there exists $p \in \mathcal{L}$, $p \neq 0$, that separates G from $\{w \in R^n : w \ll -g\}$.

Therefore,

$$\inf p \cdot G \geq \sup\{p \cdot w : w \ll -z\} = -p \cdot z = -\frac{M}{m}.$$

Since $0 \in G(t)$ for all t

$$0 \geq \frac{1}{m} \sum_T \inf p \cdot G(t) = \inf p \cdot G \geq -\frac{M}{m}.$$

Since $X(t) - I(t) + e/m \in G(t)$, for any natural number m,

$$p \cdot [X(t) - I(t)] \geq \inf p \cdot G(t).$$

If $S = \{t \in T: p \cdot [X(t) - I(t)] < 0\}$, then

$$\frac{1}{m} \sum_{S} p \cdot [X(t) - I(t)] \geq \frac{1}{m} \sum_{S} \inf p \cdot G(t) \geq -\frac{M}{m}.$$

Because

$$\frac{1}{m} \sum_{T} p \cdot [X(t) - I(t)] = \frac{1}{m} p \cdot [\sum_{T} X(t) - \Sigma I(t)] = p \cdot 0 = 0.$$

Therefore,

$$\frac{1}{m} \sum_{T} |p \cdot [X(t) - I(t)]| = \frac{2}{m} \sum_{S} |p \cdot [X(t) - I(t)]| \geq \frac{2M}{m}$$

and

$$\frac{1}{m} \sum_{T} |\inf\{p \cdot [x - I(t)]: x \} X(t)\}|$$

$$\leq -\frac{1}{m} \sum_{T} \inf p \cdot G(t) + \frac{1}{m} \sum_{t \notin S} p \cdot [X(t) - I(t)]$$

$$\leq \frac{M}{m} + \frac{M}{m} = \frac{2M}{m}.$$

Q.E.D.

12

Comparing Measure-Theoretic and Nonstandard Methods

This chapter shows that, for a significant number of questions about large economies, measure-theoretic and nonstandard methods give rise to equivalent answers; it does so by showing how to convert a given measure-theoretic economy into a nonstandard economy and vice versa. The results, however, are not proved in fullest generality. Thus Brown's procedure for converting a measure-theoretic economy into a nonstandard economy has been used only for the countably additive case; similarly, the converse result has been demonstrated only for the case when agents' characteristics come from a compact set. The references will guide the reader to the more general result.

The conclusion of this chapter attempts to evaluate the relative merits of the two approaches and may be read independently of the rest of the chapter. It is, of necessity, more polemical than anything else in this monograph. For this reason, it is important here to emphasize that the measure theorists have been the first to point out the significant questions and to devise several of the basic analytical tools for these problems.

In the introductory chapter I discussed the motivation underlying a study of economies with an infinite number of traders. I also pointed out there that there were essentially two methods for dealing with such economies: the first uses the tools of measure theory and the second those of nonstandard analysis. The relationship between nonstandard economies and measurable economies is the topic of this chapter.

The first two sections are taken up with the possibility of transforming each type of economy into an equivalent counterpart of the other. In the second section, for example, a nonstandard economy will be transformed into an (economically) equivalent measure-theoretic economy. The third section then considers the asymptotics of the two methods and provides conditions under which results proved by one method for families of large, finite economies could also have been proved by the other method. The final section asks what happens if we use the transformations of the first two sections in succession. In other words, suppose we transform a measure-theoretic economy ξ into an appropriate nonstandard economy $*\xi$ by the procedure of the first section; then transform $*\xi$ into a measure-theoretic economy $\bar{\xi}$ by the method of the second section. What can we now say about the relationship between ξ and $\bar{\xi}$? Finally, it can be argued that even though conditions for the equivalence of the two methods can be found, nonstandard analysis nonetheless possesses some distinct advantages over measure theory in its ability to formulate economically interesting infinite economies. This is the burden of the concluding section. Several mathematical and economic results which are needed only for this chapter are gathered together in the Mathematical Appendix to this chapter.

The Basic Equivalence Theorem

The equivalence between nonstandard and measure-theoretic economies involves two distinct questions. On one hand, given a measure-theoretic economy, we have to associate with it a nonstandard economy, which is, in a sense to be made precise, equivalent to the original measure-theoretic economy. On the other hand, given a nonstandard economy, we have to find a measure-theoretic economy whose economic behavior is equivalent to that of the original nonstandard economy. The pioneering work in this field is an important early contribution of Brown (1973). Not only did Brown derive a nonstandard economy from a measure-theoretic economy, he did so for the case of finitely additive measure-theoretic economies. From the mathematical point of view, this was a considerable result because it permitted us to deal with economies that have a countable number of traders, a case that had been beyond the reach of countably additive measure theory. In recent years, however, there have been standard models of agents with a countable number of traders, and the tools for dealing with finitely additive measures have also been considerably strengthened. Finitely additive economies are no longer the sole prerogative of nonstandard methods.[1] Unfortunately, the economic interpretation

1. Although the earliest equivalence results for finitely additive exchange economies were obtained by Brown (1973), the existence proof used by Brown wrongly invokes the analogue of the Schmeidler-Fatou lemma. This mistake has been pointed out, and sharper results for finitely additive economies have been provided by Armstrong and Richter (1983). In this case, the measure-theoretic results came after the nonstandard results.

of economies with a countable number of agents is somewhat suspect: for technical reasons, we cannot let all agents have equal weight, but then how do we choose the unequal weights that some agents must receive? Because of the difficulty of interpreting such economies, finitely additive measures will not be emphasized in the following presentation.

To be more specific, Brown showed that, given a measurable economy in which the agents' characteristics are chosen from a compact set, one can construct from it a nonstandard economy, its nonstandard representation, such that

1. An allocation is in the core of the measurable economy if and only if the nonstandard representation of the allocation is in the core of the nonstandard economy.
2. The core of the measurable economy is nonempty if and only if the core of the nonstandard economy is nonempty.

Brown begins with a purely competitive finitely additive measurable exchange economy $\xi' = \langle A, G, \tau, \lambda, I\rangle$, where

A is a nonempty set, the set of agents;
G is an algebra of subsets of A, the set of permissible coalitions;
τ is a nonatomic finitely additive probability measure on G; $\tau(E)$ is the fraction of traders belonging to $E \in G$. τ is nonatomic if for every $\epsilon > 0$ there exists a finite measurable partition of A, such that each set in the partition has measure less than ϵ.
λ is a Borel-measurable function from A to P, the space of preferences, with compact range. $\lambda(a)$ is the preference relation of agent a, denoted $\succ_a$.
I is a bounded Borel-measurable function from A into R^n_+. $I(a)$ is the initial endowment of agent a.

By modifying Brown's model to apply only to the countably additive case, we shall obtain a considerable simplification of Brown's original proofs.

An *allocation* X is a τ-integrable function from A into $^*R^n$ such that $\int_A X d\tau \leq \int_A I d\tau$.

A *nonnegligible coalition* is a set $S \in G$ such that $\tau(S) > 0$. An allocation Y *blocks* an allocation X via a coalition S if

(i) $\tau(S) > 0$, i.e., S is nonnegligible.
(ii) $(\forall a \in S)$, $Y(a) \succ_a X(a)$.
(iii) $\int_S Y d\tau \leq \int_S I d\tau$.

The core of ξ, $\zeta(\xi)$ is the set of unblocked allocations. Price systems or price vectors are vectors in the unit simplex of R^n and will be denoted p. The *budget set* $B_p(a)$ for agent a is

$$B_p(a) = \{x \in R^n | p \cdot x \leq p \cdot I(a)\}$$

A *competitive equilibrium* is a triple $\langle X, p, K \rangle$ such that $K \in G$, $\mu(K) = 1$; X is an allocation; $X(a)$ is maximal in $B_p(a)$ with respect to $\succ_a$. $y \succ_a X(a)$ implies $p \cdot y > p \cdot I(a)$. If $\langle X, p, K \rangle$ is a competitive equilibrium, then X is called a competitive allocation, and p a competitive price system. $\zeta_e(\xi)$ denotes the set of *competitive allocations.*

To form a nonstandard economy on ξ', Brown considers the family F of all finite measurable partitions of $\langle A, G \rangle$ ordered by refinement—that is, if $\Pi_1, \Pi_2, \epsilon F$ and Π_2 is finer than Π_1, write $\Pi_1 < \Pi_2$. $\langle {}^*A, {}^*G \rangle$ denotes the nonstandard extension of $\langle A, G \rangle$ and is assumed to be contained in a comprehensive enlargement.

Brown then uses some results of an article by Peter Loeb (1972), who has shown the existence of a partition $\Pi \in {}^*F$ such that ${}^*\Pi_0 \leq \Pi$ for all $\Pi^0 \in F$—that is, there exist $\omega_\Pi \in {}^*N - N$ and an internal bijection from $T = \{t \in {}^*N | 1 \leq t \leq \omega_\Pi\}$ onto Π. Thus we may write $\Pi = \{A_t | t \in T\}$. The A_t are all disjoint subsets of ${}^*A$ and for any $B \in G$, ${}^*B = \{A_t | A_t \subseteq {}^*B\}$. Let c_Π be a fixed internal mapping of T into ${}^*A$ such that for each $t \in T$, $c_\Pi(t) \in A_t$. Hereafter, both Π and c_Π will be fixed.

Brown defines the nonstandard representation $\tilde{\xi} = \langle T, M, \tilde{\tau}, \tilde{\lambda}, \tilde{I} \rangle$ of $\xi = \langle A, G, \tau, \lambda, I \rangle$ as follows:

T, the set of agents, is the index set for the partition $\Pi = \{A_t | t \in T\}$.

M, the set of permissible coalitions, is the family of internal subsets of T.

$\tilde{\tau}(t) = {}^*\tau(A_t)$, for all $t \in T$; $\tilde{\tau}(t)$ represents the weight assigned to trader t.

$\tilde{\lambda}(t) = {}^*\lambda[c_\Pi(t)]$, for all $t \in T$; $\tilde{\lambda}(t)$ represents the preference of agent t.

$\tilde{I}(t) = {}^*I[c_\Pi(t)]$, for all $t \in T$; $\tilde{I}(t)$ represents the initial endowment of agent t.

The nonstandard representation of an allocation X in ξ' is $\tilde{X}$, where $\tilde{X}(t) = {}^*X[c_\Pi(t)]$, for all $t \in T$. Note that ξ'_ω depends on Π and c_Π; Brown's theorem is valid for all Π and c_Π chosen in internal fashion. Loeb (1972) also establishes the following properties of measures and measurable functions on the *partitioned space:

(1) If $g: A \to M$, where M is a compact metric space and g is Borel-measurable, then g is essentially constant on each A_t, that is, $(\forall A_t \in \Pi)(\forall a, b \in A_t)$, ${}^*g(a) \simeq {}^*g(b)$.

(2) If ν is a finitely additive scalar-valued probability measure on $\langle A, G \rangle$, then for any bounded Borel-measurable function

$f{:}A \to R^n$, $\int_B f d\nu \simeq \Sigma_{t \in T_B} {}^*f(c_\Pi(t)){}^*\nu(A_t)$.
where T_B is the set of t such that ${}^*B = \{\cup A_t | t \in T_B\}$.

Before turning to the definitions of allocation and equilibrium for ξ it is helpful to try to picture the construction so as to see why we have to employ a slightly stronger equilibrium notion than before.

The procedure for obtaining a nonstandard economy can be heuristically described by considering the set of traders for the measure-theoretic economy to be identical with the set of points in the interval [0, 1]. To each point in the unit interval we attached a preference relation, $\succ_t$, and an initial endowment, $I(t)$. Allocations will be suitable functions from [0, 1] to R^n_+. Call this economy ξ. The first step consists of obtaining the nonstandard extension of ξ, denoted by ${}^*\xi$. All properties of ξ hold true for ${}^*\xi$, and ${}^*\xi$ will therefore play an important role in all our proofs. But because ξ has a standardly infinite number of traders, ${}^*\xi$ will possess a *infinite number of traders. To obtain a *finite number of traders we will have to "chop up" *[0, 1] into a "large" number of *finite intervals and identify each interval with a trader. It may be useful to picture the process graphically. We start off with all the points in [0, 1]. When we move to ${}^*\xi$ we add many new points. For each real number r in [0, 1] we add a monad of infinitesimals around r. This makes the number of traders very much larger, of course, but since we have only used transfer so far all properties of ξ are still true. Now we chop up [0, 1]* into an infinite number of small intervals, say, of width $1/\omega$ each, where $\omega \in {}^*R - R$. The monad around a point r contains many such intervals—infinitely many intervals of length $1/\omega$—so one should not think that we are simply back to [0, 1] by taking the equivalence class of monads around each real number in [0, 1]. So the situation is somewhat as in figure 8. Let ξ_ω denote the *finite economy. Now if each (infinitesimal) interval is to be one trader, we must use an equilibrium notion that is robust to infinitesimal changes. Otherwise, each infinitesimal interval representing one trader may react to a given stimulus in two ways, and our models cannot handle such schizophrenia. The requirement that each infinitesimal interval have uniquely defined behavior naturally leads us to use the Brown-Robinson (monadic) equilibrium as our equilibrium concept. We now return to providing the rest of our definitions.

An *allocation* is a standardly bounded internal function X from T into ${}^*R_n$ such that

$$\sum_{t \in T} X(t)\mu(t) \simeq \sum_{t \in T} I(t)\mu(t).$$

A *nonnegligible coalition* is a set $E \in M$, such that $\mu(E) \gtrsim 0$.

An allocation X *blocks* an allocation Y, if there exists a nonnegligible coalition E such that

$$\sum_{t\in E} X(t)\mu(t) \simeq \sum_{t\in E} I(t)\mu(t)$$

and $(\forall t \in E)X(t) \}\}_t Y(t)$, where $w \}\}_t z$ iff $\forall v \simeq w$, $\forall u \simeq z$, $v \}_t u$.

The *core* of $\tilde{\xi}$, $\zeta(\tilde{\xi})$, is the set of unblocked allocations.

Price systems or price vectors are vectors in the unit simplex of $*R^n$ and will be denoted p.

The *budget set* $B_p(t)$ for the tth trader is $B_p(t) = \{x \in *R_n | p \cdot x \leq p \cdot I(t)\}$.

A *competitive equilibrium* is a triple $\langle X, p, K \rangle$ such that $K \in T$ $\mu(K) \simeq 1$; X is an allocation; $X(t)$ is maximal in $B_p(t)$ with respect to $\}\}_t$ for all $t \in K$. To say that $X(t)$ is maximal in $B_p(t)$ means $X(t) \in B_p(t)$ and $(\forall y \in *R^n_+)y \}\}_t X(t) \Rightarrow p \cdot y \gneq p \cdot I(t)$. If $\langle X, p, K \rangle$ is a competitive equilibrium, then X is called a competitive allocation and p is called a competitive price system or competitive prices. $\zeta_e(\tilde{\xi})$ denotes the set of competitive allocations.

A preference relation $\} \in *P$ is said to be *S-monotone* if $^ox \} ^oy$, then $x \} \}_t y$.

It must be repeated that although the derivation of a nonstandard economy from a measure-theoretic economy has followed Brown's original construction, to prove our results we shall strengthen the hypothesis from finitely additive to countably additive measures.

We have three economies to deal with: ξ, a standard measure-theoretic economy with a countably additive measure; $*\xi$, the nonstandard extension of ξ; and $\tilde{\xi}$, the nonstandard representation of $*\xi$ obtained by using the Loeb representation. Brown and Robinson (1974) prove an equivalence theorem between cores and competitive equilibria using the above definitions.

THEOREM 1. *X is in the core of* ξ, $\zeta(\xi)$, *if* $\tilde{X}$ *is in the core of* ξ, $\zeta(\tilde{\xi})$.

PROOF. If $X \notin \zeta(\xi)$, then there exists an assignment $Y(t)$ and a coalition S such that

1. $\nu(S) > 0$.
2. $Y(t) \} X(t)$, for all t in S.
3. $\int Y(t)d\nu = \int I(t)d\nu$.

Now 1 implies $\mu(*S) \gneq 0$, and 2 implies $\tilde{Y}(t) \}\} \tilde{X}(t)$, while from Loeb's theorem and 3 we have

$$\sum \tilde{Y}(t)\mu(t) = \int Y(t)d\nu = \int I(t)d\nu \simeq \sum \tilde{I}(t)\mu(t)$$

So $\tilde{Y}(t)$ is an assignment blocking $\tilde{X}(t)$. Q.E.D.

REMARK 1. The condition that $\mu(E) > 0$ for a blocking coalition would have sufficed for the above proof. We could not relax $Y(t) \succ\succ X(t)$ to $Y(t) \succ X(t)$, however, because we could have $Y(t) \succ X(t)$ and yet ${}^oY(t) \not\succ {}^oX(t)$. Only the condition that $Y(t) \succ\succ X(t)$ will suffice to guarantee that when we move from $Y(t)$ to $^*Y(t)$ and from $X(t)$ to $^*X(t)$ we can still claim that $^*Y(t) \succ {}^*X(t)$, that is, the condition on preference must be strong enough to sustain a "flattening out" of the function $Y(t)$ and $X(t)$ over A_t.

We now have core $\tilde{\xi} \neq \emptyset$ implies core $\xi \neq \emptyset$. To show that core $\xi \neq \emptyset$ implies core $\tilde{\xi} \neq \emptyset$ we shall follow the indirect route of showing that $\zeta_e(\xi) \neq \emptyset$ implies $\zeta_e(\tilde{\xi}) \neq \emptyset$, and rely on the equivalence theorems already proved for measure-theoretic economies, such as Aumann (1964).

THEOREM 2. *If* (X, p) *is in* $\zeta_e(\xi)$ *then* $(\tilde{X}, \tilde{p})$ *is in* $\zeta_e(\tilde{\xi})$.

PROOF. Since $\tilde{\xi}$ is a bona fide countably additive measure theoretic economy, we know—see, for example Schmeidler (1969)—that $\zeta_e(\tilde{\xi}) \neq \phi$. Now (X, p) in $\zeta(\xi)$ means that

(i) $\forall a \in K$, with $\tau(K) = 1$, $X(a)$ is maximal in $B_p(a)$.
(ii) $\int X d\tau \leq \int I d\tau$.

Let K' denote the set of traders in T who arise in the representation of X, denoted $\tilde{X}$. Then $\tau(K) = 1$ implies $\mu(K') \simeq 1$.

If $\tilde{X}(t)$ is not maximal in $B_{\tilde{p}}(t)$, then there exists $y \in {}^*R^n$ such that $Y \succ\succ_t \tilde{X}(t)$ and $\tilde{p} \cdot Y \lesssim \tilde{p} \cdot I(t)$. But this in turn implies that $Y \succ_a {}^o[\tilde{X}(t)]$ and $p \cdot Y \leq p \cdot I(t)$, which contradicts (i) above. Hence $\tilde{X}(t)$ is maximal in $B_{\tilde{p}}(t)$. Finally, from property (2) of the Loeb representation (quoted above) it follows from (ii) that $1/\omega\ \Sigma_T \tilde{X}(t) \simeq 1/\omega\ \Sigma_T \tilde{I}(t)$. Q.E.D.

From Nonstandard Economies to Measure-Theoretic Economies

The major difference between the measure-theoretic representation of a nonstandard economy, to be exposited now, and Brown's nonstandard representation of a measure-theoretic economy is that in the representation of this section, the set of traders in the nonstandard economy is identical with the set of traders in its measure-theoretic representation. This identity enables us to obtain somewhat stronger results in this section.

We are given a nonstandard exchange economy—a 5-tuple $\tilde{\xi} = \langle T, \phi, \nu, I, \rho \rangle$ corresponding to the set of traders, permissible coalitions, and the like, and we are to form from those $\tilde{\xi}$ a measure-theoretic ${}^o\xi$, which will be another 5-tuple whose elements are defined analogously to those of $\tilde{\xi}$. Loeb (1975) is of critical importance below. (See Appendix for definitions and results.) We form ${}^o\xi$ as follows:

A. Map each individual of $\tilde{\xi}$ onto himself in ${}^o\xi$ by the identity mapping—the set of traders remains unchanged.
B. Extend the set of permissible coalitions from α, the algebra of internal subsets of T, to the standard σ-algebra M on T defined by Loeb's procedure for converting nonstandard measure spaces into standard measure spaces.
C. Similarly, use the Loeb procedure to extend the nonstandard infinitesimal measure ν on ϕ to a nonatomic standard measure on M.
D. Assign the standard part of each individual's initial endowment onto his counterpart in ${}^o\xi$—move from $I(t)$ to ${}^o[I(t)]$. This is well defined since each initial endowment $I(t)$ is standardly bounded and hence all standard parts exist. This assignment is M-measurable by Theorem 2.
E. Assign the standard part of each individual's preference in $\tilde{\xi}$ onto his counterpart in ${}^o\xi$—map $\}_t \rightarrow {}^o\}_t$. Lemma 1 tells us that such standard parts exist (all preferences are required to lie in a compact subset of $*P$) and that ${}^o\}_t$ is continuous in R^n under the conditions we have imposed on $\}_t$. Since Hildenbrand (1972) has shown that the space of preferences is a complete, separable metric space, the extension of Theorem 2 further tells us that if the original assignment of individuals to preferences was internal and σ-measurable, then the new assignment of individuals to preferences will be M-measurable.

THEOREM 3. *X is in the core of $\tilde{\xi}$, $\zeta(\tilde{\xi})$, if and only if ${}^oX$ is in the core of ${}^o\xi$, $\zeta({}^o\xi)$.*

PROOF. Suppose $X \notin \zeta(\tilde{\xi})$, $\rightarrow \exists Y(t)$, $t \in R$ with $\nu(R) \gtrsim\!\!\!\!/\; 0$, such that

1. $Y \} \}_t X$, and

2. $\sum_R Yd\nu \simeq \sum_R Id\nu$.

Now $Y \} \} X \rightarrow {}^oY\, {}^o\}\, {}^oX$ by Lemma 1, and using Theorem 3 twice,

$$\int_R {}^oYd\mu \simeq \sum_R Yd\nu$$

$$\int_R {}^oId\mu \simeq \sum_R Id\nu$$

but $\Sigma_R\, Id\nu \simeq \Sigma_R\, Yd\nu$, and the *L.H.S.* above are standard numbers

$$\therefore \int_R {}^oY d\mu = \int_R {}^oI d\mu.$$

Hence ${}^oY\,{}^o\}_t\,{}^oX$ for all $t \in R$, with $\mu(R) > 0$ and $\int_R {}^oY d\mu = \int_R {}^oI d\mu$. Thus ${}^oY$ blocks ${}^oX$ and we have shown that $X \notin \zeta(\bar{\xi}) \to {}^oX \notin \zeta({}^o\xi)$ or, equivalently, $\nu(\bar{\xi})\zeta({}^o\xi) \subseteq \zeta(\bar{\xi})$.

We now show that core ${}^o\xi \subseteq$ core $\bar{\xi}$. Because the blocking allocations in ${}^o\xi$ can be unbounded, it turns out to be easier to show the competitive equilibria of ${}^o\xi$ to contain the competitive equilibria of ξ—that is, $\zeta_e({}^o\xi) \subseteq \zeta_e(\xi)$. Since $\zeta_e({}^o\xi) = \zeta({}^o\xi)$ by the results of Aumann (1964), and since $\zeta_e(\bar{\xi}) = \zeta(\bar{\xi})$ by Theorem 8.1, this will suffice to complete our proof.

Suppose X is an equilibrium allocation for $\bar{\xi}$, with equilibrium price $\tilde{p}$, but that ${}^oX$ is not competitive allocation for ${}^o\xi$ with equilibrium price $p = {}^o(\tilde{p})$. Note that $p \gneqq\gneqq 0$ (Brown, 1976).

$V' = \{t \mid Y\,{}^o\}_t\,{}^oX$ and $p \cdot Y \leq p \cdot {}^oI\}$ is measurable because the assignment of endowments and preferences is measurable; since ${}^oX$ is not an equilibrium allocation, $\nu(V') > 0$.

By Lemma 1, $Y\,{}^o\}_t\,{}^oX \to Y\,\}\,\}_t\,X$ and $p \cdot Y \leq p \cdot {}^oI \to \tilde{p} \cdot Y \lesssim \tilde{p} \cdot \tilde{I}$ for all $t \in V'$

since ν is nonatomic, by Theorem 1, we can find an internal $V'' \leq V'$ such $\nu(V'') \gneqq 0$. But the existence of such a V' denies that X is an equilibrium allocation for $\bar{\xi}$, a contradiction of our original hypothesis.

THEOREM 4. *The core of the nonstandard economy $\bar{\xi}$ is nonempty if and only if the core of its representation, ${}^o\xi$, is nonempty—that is, $\zeta(\bar{\xi}) \neq \emptyset \leftrightarrow \zeta({}^o\xi) \neq \emptyset$.*

PROOF. We have already shown above that $\zeta(\bar{\xi}) \neq \emptyset \to \zeta({}^o\xi) \neq \emptyset$. We have now to show that $Y \in \zeta({}^o\xi)$ implies the existence of an $X \in \zeta(\bar{\xi})$.

Since $\zeta({}^o\xi) = \zeta_e({}^o\xi)$, as proved by Aumann (1964), $Y \in \zeta_e({}^o\xi)$. Let p denote the associated equilibrium price. Schmeidler (1969) has shown that all equilibrium prices are positive in all components. Let the minimal component be p^j.

For any trader, $p^jY^j \leq p \cdot Y \leq p \cdot I \leq r$, where r is the uniform bound on the initial endowments.

Thus $Y^j \leq r/p^j$ and $Y^i \leq r/p^i < r/p^j$ and Y is uniformly bounded—that is, $Y \leq r/p^j \cdot e$.

By Proposition 1 of the Mathematical Appendix to this chapter, there exists an internal ${}^*Y : T \to {}^*R^n_+$, such that ${}^o({}^*Y) = Y$ almost everywhere with respect to μ. If $^*Y$ is not an equilibrium allocation for ξ, then, by Theorem 3, Y cannot be an equilibrium allocation for $^o\xi$, a contradiction of our original hypothesis.

Hence $Y \in \zeta(^o\xi) = \zeta_e(^o\xi) \rightarrow {}^*Y \in \zeta(\bar{\xi}) = \zeta_e(\bar{\xi})$.

Asymptotic Equivalence

The study of economies with an infinite number of traders has been largely motivated by a desire to obtain results about the behavior of large but finite economies. It is thus interesting to ask in just what sense we can speak of a sequence of finite economies tending to a limit economy. Since the domains of these economies—the number of agents—keep on increasing, it is clear that no direct definition will suffice. Werner Hildenbrand (1970a), following earlier work by Kannai (1970), suggested that the proper concept was to speak of the proportion of consumers in each economy who shared a common preference and endowment. Since all our agents map into the same space of preferences and endowments regardless of the size of the economy, this leads us directly to the concept of convergence in distribution.

Mathematically, the situation may be expressed as follows: We have a sequence of measure spaces, $\langle A_n, \alpha_n, \nu_n, f_n\rangle$, $n = 0, 1, 2 \ldots$ where A_n is a set (the set of agents in economic terms); α_n is a σ-algebra on A_n (the set of permissible coalitions); and ν_n is a measure on α_n (the weight of an individual or coalition). Each measure space maps into a compact metric space V (the Cartesian product of endowment and preference space) via the measurable mapping f_n. If β is the σ-algebra of Borel sets on V, then the induced measure ν_{f_n} on V for each member of the sequence $\langle A_n, \alpha_n, \nu_n, f_n\rangle$ is defined as

$$\nu_{f_n}(B) = \nu_n \cdot f_n^{-1}(B), \qquad \forall B \in \beta.$$

We say that the sequence of economies represented by $\langle A_n, \alpha_n, \nu_n, f_n\rangle$ tends to the economy represented by $\langle A_o, \alpha_o, \nu_o, f_o\rangle$ if

$$\nu_{f_n} \xrightarrow{\text{weak}} \nu_{f_o}$$

That is, for all bounded and continuous functions h from V into R,

$$\int_V h d\nu_{f_n} \rightarrow \int_V h d\nu_{f_o}.$$

An equivalent statement of the above is that the f_n *converge in distribution* to f_o.

Let ξ_n denote the economy $\langle A_n, \alpha_n, \nu_n, f_n \rangle$ for all $n = 0, 1, 2, \ldots$ In terms of our earlier definitions $f_n = (I_n, \succ_n)$, for all n. If V is any subset of $P \times R^n$, then a sequence of economies $\{\xi_n\}$ with characteristics in V is said to be *purely competitive* on V if

(a) The number of agents in ξ_n, $|A_n|$, tends to infinity.
(b) The sequence of preference-endowment distributions converges weakly on V—that is,

$$\nu_{f_n} \xrightarrow{\text{weak}} \nu_{f_o}.$$

(c) $$\lim_{n\to\infty} \int I_o d\nu_{f_n} = \int I_o d\nu_{f_o}.$$

(d) $$\int I_o d\nu_{f_o} \gg 0.$$

This definition is taken from Hildenbrand (1974). Purely competitive sequences of economies form that class of finite economies whose behavior at infinity enables us to deduce aspects of their behavior for large finite n—that is, properties of ξ_o are reflected in corresponding properties of ξ_n, for large n.

Since we can extend the sequence of finite economies forming a purely competitive sequence into a family of nonstandard economies $\{\xi_n\}_{n\in{}^*N}$, we would like to know how the property of arising from a purely competitive sequence is reflected in the ξ_ω, $\omega \in {}^*N - N$. Consider the extensions of our measure spaces to the nonstandard integers—that is, $\langle A_\omega, \alpha_\omega, \nu_\omega, f_\omega \rangle$, for $\omega \in {}^*N - N$ and the corresponding extensions ${}^*V$, ${}^*\beta$. Then our first problem is to find a nonstandard characterization of weak convergence. We shall prove the following theorem.

THEOREM 5. $\nu_{f_n} \xrightarrow{\text{weak}} \nu_{f_o}$ *if and only if* $\nu_{f_o} = \mu_{{}^of_\omega}$, $\omega \in {}^*N - N$, *where* ${}^of_\omega ; A_\omega \to V$, *is defined by* ${}^of_\omega(a) = {}^o(f_\omega(a))$, $\forall a \in A_\omega$, *and* $\mu_{{}^of_\omega}$ *is the Loeb measure derived from* ν_{f_ω}.

PROOF. We wish to show that $\nu_{f_o} = \mu_{{}^of_\omega}$, $\forall \omega \in {}^*N - N$. By the Riesz representation theorem (see Royden, 1963), this is equivalent to showing that for all bounded and continuous $h: V \to R$,

$$\int_V h d\mu_{{}^of_\omega} = \int_V h d\nu_{f_o}, \qquad \forall \omega \in {}^*N - N. \tag{1}$$

By the change of variables theorem for integrals, for any $\omega \in {}^*N - N$,

$$\int_V h d\mu_{{}^of_\omega} = \int_{A_\omega} h \cdot {}^of_\omega d\mu_\omega \quad \text{and} \quad \int_V h d\nu_{f_o} = \int_{A_\omega} h \cdot f_o d\nu_o. \tag{2}$$

Hence what we have to show is equivalent to

$$\int_{A_\omega} h \cdot {}^o f_\omega d\mu_\omega = \int_{A_\omega} h \cdot f_o d\nu_o .$$

By transfer of the fact that μ_{f_n} converge weakly to μ_{f_o}, for all bounded, continuous $h : V \to R$,

$$\int_{A_o} h \cdot f_o d\nu_o \simeq \int_{A_\omega} {}^*h \cdot f_\omega d\nu_\omega, \qquad \forall \omega \in {}^*N - N, \tag{3}$$

($^*h$ is the nonstandard extension of h). How does

$$\int_{A_\omega} {}^*h \cdot f_\omega d\nu_\omega$$

compare with

$$\int_{A_\omega} h \cdot {}^o f_\omega d\mu_\omega ?$$

We note that $^*h \cdot f_\omega$ is α_ω-measurable and that $h \cdot {}^o f_\omega$ is M-measurable, where M is the Loeb σ-algebra on A_ω. Let $g = {}^*h \cdot f_\omega$. If we can show that ${}^o g = h \cdot {}^o f_\omega$, we can appeal to Theorem 3 of the Appendix to this chapter. Since h is bounded, so is $^*h$ and all the conditions of the theorem will be fulfilled.

$\forall a \in A_\omega$, $f_\omega(a) \simeq {}^o f_\omega(a)$, and since h is continuous $^*h \cdot f_\omega(a) \simeq {}^*h \cdot {}^o f_\omega(a) \simeq h \cdot {}^o f_\omega(a)$, . . .—that is, ${}^o g = h \cdot {}^o f_\omega$.

By Theorem 3 of the Appendix we have

$$\int_{A_\omega} {}^*h \cdot f_\omega d\nu_\omega = \int_{A_\omega} g d\nu_\omega \simeq \int_{A_\omega} {}^o g d\mu_\omega = \int_{A_\omega} h \cdot {}^o f_\omega d\mu_\omega . \tag{4}$$

Combining our results, we have, for all bounded, continuous $h : V \to R$,

$$\int_{A_o} h \cdot f_o d\nu_o \simeq \int_{A_\omega} h \cdot {}^o f_\omega d\nu_\omega \simeq \int_{A_\omega} h \cdot {}^o f_\omega d\mu_\omega, \ \forall \omega \in {}^*N - N. \tag{5}$$

But both the first and last terms are standard numbers, hence

$$\int_{A_o} h \cdot f_o d\nu_o = \int_{A_\omega} h \cdot {}^o f_\omega d\mu_\omega, \qquad \forall \omega \in {}^*N - N, \tag{6}$$

that is,

$$\nu_{f_o} = \mu_{{}^o f_\omega}, \qquad \forall \omega \in {}^*N - N.$$

This proves necessity.

To prove sufficiency, we start with

$$\nu_{f_0} = \mu_{{}^o f_\omega}, \qquad \forall \omega \in {}^*N - N,$$

and note that it implies (6). But each step in the above proof is "reversible," that is, (6) → (5) → (4) → (3) → (2) → (1), which is what we need to prove sufficiency. Q.E.D.

Having obtained a nonstandard characterization of weak convergence, we are now ready to provide a nonstandard characterization of purely competitive sequences. Let $\{\xi_n\}_{n\in{}^*N}$ denote a family of nonstandard economies, where $\xi_n = \langle A_n, \alpha_n, \nu_n, f_n\rangle$, and each f_n is a measurable mapping of A_n into $^*V$, the nonstandard extension of a compact subset of the Cartesian product of endowment and preference space—that is, $f_n = (I_n, \succ_n)$ as previously defined.

THEOREM 6. *$\{\xi_n\}_{n\in{}^*N}$ represents a purely competitive sequence of economies if and only if*

(i) *The number of traders in ξ_n, $|A_n|$, tends to infinity.*
(ii) $\nu_{f_0} = \mu_{{}^o f_\omega}$, $\forall \omega \in {}^*N - N$.
(iii) *I_ω is S-integrable for all $\omega \in {}^*N - N$.*
(iv) $\int {}^oI_\omega d\mu_{{}^o f_\omega} \gg 0$, *for all $\omega \in {}^*N - N$.*

PROOF. We have to show that the conditions (a), (b), (c), and (d) in the earlier-stated definition of a purely competitive sequence are equivalent to conditions (i), (ii), (iii) and (iv) above.

(a) and (i) are obviously identical.
(b) and (ii) were shown to be identical in Theorem 5 above.

Before showing the equivalence of (c) and (iii), and (d) and (iv), we shall need a further definition and theorem. Let f_n be a sequence of measurable functions from $\langle A_n, \alpha_n, \nu_n\rangle$ into R^n. The following definition and result are taken from Hildenbrand (1974):

The sequence $\{f_n\}_{n\in N}$ is said to be *uniformly integrable* if

$$\lim_{q\to\infty}\left(\sup_n \int_{|f_n|>q} |f_n| d\nu_n\right) = 0$$

THEOREM 7. *Let the sequence $\{f_n\}$ of measurable functions converge in distribution to the measurable function f. If the sequence $\{f_n\}$ is uniformly integrable, then f is integrable and*

$$\lim_n \int f_n d\nu_n = \int f d\nu$$

(c) and (iii) are seen to be equivalent if we successively set $f_n = I_o$ and $f_n = {}^oI_\omega$ for all n; since both I_o and ${}^oI_\omega$ are bounded functions, the sequences are uniformly integrable, and Theorem 7 applies.

(d) states that $\int I_o d\nu_{f_o} \gg 0$. f_n converges in distribution to f_o by (b) and since $f_n = (I_n, \lambda_n)$ it follows that I_n converges in distribution to I_o since these distributions are the marginal distributions of f_n and f_0. By Theorem 7 it follows that $\int I_n d\nu_{f_n} \gg 0$ for all large n. But then we must have $\int I_\omega d\nu_{f_\omega} \not\gg 0$, for all $\omega \in {}^*N - N$, and by Theorem 3 of the Appendix

$$\int {}^oI_\omega d\mu_{{}^of_\omega} \gg 0.$$

Similarly,

$$\int {}^oI_\omega d\mu_{{}^of_\omega} \gg 0$$

implies

$$\int I_n d\nu_{f_n} \gg 0$$

for all large n, which in turn implies that

$$\int I_o d\nu_{f_o} \gg 0.$$

This completes the proof.

In deducing characteristics of large but finite economies from the behavior of economies with infinitely many traders, measure-theoretic and nonstandard methods are apparently quite different. In the measure-theoretic methodology, results are stated in terms of a special class of large, finite economies—the purely competitive sequences—and the theory of weak convergence is then used. In the nonstandard method, conditions are placed on the endowments and preferences of all finite economies so that the nonstandard extension of the finite economies—that is, ξ_ω, $\omega \in {}^*N - N$, will satisfy the conditions under which, for example, equilibrium exists. It can then be shown that since an equilibrium exists for all ξ_ω, an approximate equilibrium must exist for all ξ_n. In contrast to the measure-theoretic formulation, nothing is said about the preference endowment distributions of the finite economies ξ_n. The following two theorems, which are adapted from Hildenbrand (1974), will show that for nonstandard economies with compact characteristics, the two methods are equivalent because the assumptions made on the sequence of large but finite economies in the nonstandard framework are such as to imply that the sequence possesses a purely competitive subsequence, which is what is required in the measure-theoretic framework.

We require a definition. A family of measures M on a metric space T is called *tight* if for every $\epsilon > 0$ there exists a compact set $K \subseteq T$ such that $\mu(K) > 1 - \epsilon$ for every $\mu \in M$.

THEOREM 8. *If the sequence of functions f_n is uniformly integrable, then the sequence of distributions of f_n, ν_{f_n} is tight.*

THEOREM 9. *If the family of measures, M, is tight, then every sequence of measures in M contains a weakly converging subsequence.*

Since our preferences and endowments are chosen from fixed compact subsets of the respective spaces, the functions f_n are uniformly integrable and the family of induced measures ν_{f_n} is tight by Theorem 8. Therefore, by Theorem 9 there exists a weakly convergent subsequence, as required in the definition of a purely competitive sequence. This covers conditions (b) and (c) in the definition of a purely competitive sequence. That condition (d) also holds has been shown earlier in the chapter. This demonstrates that the conditions under which nonstandard limit theorems have been proved are equivalent to those under which measure-theoretic limit theorems have been proved (with compactness assumed).

From Measure-Theoretic to Nonstandard and Back

Brown (1973) derived a nonstandard exchange economy $\bar{\xi}_\omega$ from a given measure-theoretic economy ξ; we have derived a measure-theoretic economy ${}^o\xi$ from an arbitrary nonstandard exchange economy $\bar{\xi}$. An obvious question is whether ξ would be economically equivalent to ${}^o\xi$ in any way if we pick $\bar{\xi} = \bar{\xi}_\omega$. We denote the measure-theoretic economy derived from $\bar{\xi}_\omega$ via the Loeb construction by ${}^o\xi_\omega$ and note that since ${}^o\xi_\omega$ is a bona fide atomless economy in the sense of Hildenbrand, we can apply known results about measure-theoretic atomless economies directly to ${}^o\xi_\omega$. We shall show that $\zeta_e(\xi) \neq \emptyset$ if and only if $\zeta_e({}^o\xi_\omega) \neq \emptyset$.

Hildenbrand (1974) has shown that ξ may be considered as the limit of a sequence of finite economies $\{\xi_n\}$ in the sense that the preference-endowment distributions of the ξ_n converge weakly to the preference-endowment distribution of ξ. The ξ_n are constructed from a sequence L_n of finite, Borel-measurable partitions of V, the preference-endowment space of ξ, which, by assumption, is a compact subset of $P \times R_n$; the partitions

$\{L_n\}$ are assumed to get successively finer—that is, L_m is a refinement of L_n for all $m \geq n$. We note that if we extend the sequence of partitions $\{L_n\}$ to $*N$, we obtain Loeb partitions L_ω, $\omega \in *N - N$, of $*V$, as described earlier while discussing Brown's construction.

For each n, a suitable point is chosen from each member of L_n; the collection of such chosen points then forms a finite economy ξ_n, where each trader has the weight of that member of L_n he was chosen from. Let f_n denote the function-choosing endowments and preferences for ξ_n. Since the ξ_n converge to ξ it follows that the f_n converge in distribution to f. We now note that if we extend the sequence $\langle L_n, f_n \rangle$ to $*N$, then for all $\omega \in *N - N$, L_ω is a Loeb partition of $*V$ and f_ω is an internal, bounded, and $*$Borel-measurable function—the economy ξ_ω defined by $\langle L_\omega, f_\omega \rangle$ is an economy as constructed in Brown (1973), with the only difference being that whereas the f_ω for Brown is any internal selection function from L_ω, our f_ω is such that there exists a sequence of choice functions f_n on V such that $f_n \to f_\omega$ in distribution.

Let μ and ${}^o\mu$ denote the preference-endowment distributions of ξ and ${}^o\xi$ respectively. Since the preference-endowment distributions of ξ_n converge weakly to μ, it follows from Theorem 9 that $\mu = {}^o\mu$. Since every allocation is the mapping of the set of traders, a measure space, into commodity space, it is meaningful to speak of the distribution f as an allocation. Let $D\zeta_e(\xi')$ denote the distribution of equilibrium allocations for any given economy ξ'. Under the assumptions I have made on preferences and endowments, the following theorem has been proved by Hart, Hildenbrand, and Kohlberg (1974).

THEOREM 10. *Let ξ_1 and ξ_2 be two atomless economies with $\mu_{\xi_1} = \mu_{\xi_2}$. Then $D\zeta_e(\xi_1)$ and $D\zeta_e(\xi_2)$ have the same closure with respect to weak convergence; in particular, $\zeta_e(\xi_1) \neq \emptyset$ if and only if $\zeta_e(\xi_2) \neq \emptyset$.*

But $\mu = {}^o\mu$ and hence $\zeta_e(\xi) \neq \emptyset$ if and only if $\zeta_e({}^o\xi_\omega) \neq \emptyset$.

As a corollary, we note that Theorem 4 states that $\zeta_e(\bar{\xi}_\omega) \neq \emptyset$ if and only if $\zeta_e({}^o\xi_\omega) \neq \emptyset$. This implies that $\zeta_e(\xi) \neq \emptyset$ if and only if $\zeta_e(\bar{\xi}_\omega) \neq \emptyset$.

We collect together the main results shown above in the following theorem.

THEOREM 11. *Let ξ be an atomless economy. In Hildenbrand* (1974) *it is shown that ξ may be considered as the limit of a sequence of finite economies ξ_n—the ξ_n converge weakly to ξ. Extend $\{\xi_n\}$ to $*N$. Then the following are true:*

a. *Every ξ_ω, $\omega \in *N - N$ is then a Brown representation of ξ as defined in Brown* (1973).

b. $\zeta_e(\xi) \neq \emptyset$ *if and only if* $\zeta_e({}^o\xi_\omega) \neq \emptyset$, *where* ${}^o\xi_\omega$ *is the measure-theoretic economy constructed from* ξ_ω *as described in the second section of this chapter.*

Nonstandard versus Measure-Theoretic Models

In comparing the use of nonstandard analysis with measure theory as alternative tools for describing economies with infinitely many traders it is important to begin by recognizing the important historical fact that, with the exception of results on cores with costs of coalition formation, all results of economic interest were first proved with measure theory. Even though the purist may argue that historical precedence is not a point in logic, if measure theory is a tool that most easily inspires new results, its value would be beyond debate. Once a result is known to be true, it is usually quite simple to find simpler proofs, but this does little to diminish the luster of the original discovery. Even for those who find measure theory a more intuitive tool, nonstandard analysis can nonetheless be a considerable help. Having proved a result, call it Z, for an infinite measure-theoretic economy, how are we to deduce its implications for large, finite families of economies? One very simple method is the following.

A. Formulate the nonstandard economy $^*\xi$ corresponding to the measure-theoretic economy ξ.
B. Use Loeb's method to transform $^*\xi$ into a bona fide measure-theoretic economy $\tilde{\xi}$.
C. Since Z is true for any measure-theoretic economy, it is certainly true for $\tilde{\xi}$.
D. Z being true for $\tilde{\xi}$ implies that a corresponding statement, call it Z', is true for $^*\xi$. (Since the agents in $^*\xi$ are identical with those in $\tilde{\xi}$, this involves very little work.)
E. Z' is a result true for a nonstandard economy $^*\xi$. Use the method of transfer to see what this implies about families of large, finite economies.

It is important to emphasize that the above procedure entirely obviates any need to use the theory of weak convergence of measures.

The ease with which asymptotic implications are discovered is not the only justification for the use of nonstandard analysis. It is generally very amenable to our intuition. The discoverers of the calculus, Newton and Leibniz, and later nineteenth-century mathematicians such as Augustin Cauchy, repeatedly used infinitesimals in their reasoning. The practice has certainly not ended, as a look at the seminal article by an expert measure theorist, R. J. Aumann, will show. In "Values of Markets with a Continuum of Traders," Aumann (1975) employs infinitesimals to motivate and explain the entire strategy of his proofs. Only later does measure theory enter. Certainly, then, it seems reasonable to argue that nonstandard analysis is at least as intuitive as measure theory.

In addition to providing asymptotic results easily and being readily amenable to our intuition, nonstandard economies also provide some secondary benefits. For example, it struck some economists, such as Vind (1964), at an early stage that since individuals were negligible in the measure-theoretic framework, the proper way to formulate such economies was to take coalitions and not individuals as the primitive concept. Not only does this involve us in some nice questions, such as the most meaningful definition of preferences for a coalition, it also involves trying to reconcile the two measure-theoretic approaches—the individual-based formulation of Aumann and the coalition-based approach of Vind. Although such a reconciliation can be effected, a glance at some of the mathematical questions involved, for example, in the article by Debreu (1967b), should convince most economists that one is better off using a tool within which such questions do not arise. Of course, if one insists on using the coalitional approach of Vind, this can be done within nonstandard analysis; indeed, within nonstandard economies, the consistency of the individual and coalitional approaches is readily proved.

Nonstandard analysis is particularly helpful in treating models in which individual behavior is significant. Indeed, the fact that individuals are made evanescent by fiat in any model using (nonatomic) measure theory leads to some curious results. For example, Donald John Roberts and Andrew Postlewaite (1976) asked the following question: Can an agent gain by providing the Walrasian auctioneer with a "demand" curve that is *not* generated by the agent's true utility function? For the sake of concreteness, let α be the individual who wishes to take advantage of the fact that everyone but himself will provide a truthful response at any given price. Let $ED(p)$ denote the excess demand of everyone but α at the price vector p. Then α can ensure p as an equilibrium price vector if his response $y(\alpha)$ is such that

$$ED(p) + y(\alpha) = 0. \qquad (*)$$

(Of course, $y(\alpha)$ has to be feasible for α.) Roberts and Postlewaite show by an example that it is possible to define a family of economies with increasing numbers of agents such that manipulation is not only possible in all such economies, but further that the benefits of manipulation do not decrease even in an infinite economy. This surprising result shows that individuals can have finite manipulative power even in infinite economies.

Next, Roberts and Postlewaite turn to economies with a continuum of agents and define a set of excess demands at prices p to provide an equilibrium if

$$\int_T e(t)dt = 0 \qquad (**)$$

where T is the set of agents and $e(t)$ is the excess demand of agent t at prices p. In this framework, since agent α by himself cannot affect the value of the integral, it would make no difference if we wrote

$$\int_{T/\alpha} e(t)dt + \int_{\{\alpha\}} e(\alpha)d\alpha = 0.$$

It is curious that Roberts and Postlewaite chose to model a question involving individual behavior with a mathematical tool in which individuals are, of necessity, negligible. The difference between (*) and (**) is that (*) asserts

$$\Sigma\, e(t) = 0$$

whereas (**) asserts

$$\frac{1}{k} \sum_{t=1}^{k} e(t) \rightarrow 0 \quad \text{as} \quad k \rightarrow \infty.$$

The difference between these two statements is, of course, considerable. Unfortunately, measure theory is able to handle infinite sums only by considering averages, and this technical necessity forces Roberts and Postlewaite (implicitly) to change their definitions in the course of their article. Since nonstandard analysis can handle exact equality even when infinite sums are concerned, it would appear to be a more appropriate mathematical tool for problems in which individuals can have a significant influence.

It has been argued in this section that nonstandard analysis is readily accessible to the economist's intuition, that it provides a simple, almost trivial, method of obtaining results about large, finite economies (the objects of real interest to economists), and that its use enables us to avoid a number of questions that arise naturally within measure theory but which, from the economist's point of view, can only be considered mathematical distractions. It is also the only convenient tool to use when we wish to model situations in which specified individuals are to have significant influence. Unless one happens to find measure theory an intuitively appealing way of approaching questions about economies with many agents, nonstandard analysis appears to be the more advisable mathematical tool to employ in dealing with infinite economies.

Mathematical Appendix

A. The first proposition is a nonstandard description of $\langle \mathcal{P}, \tau_c \rangle$, the spaces of preferences with the topology of closed convergence, and is taken from Brown (1973). d_p will be the metric on $\mathcal{P}$; for all $x \in {}^*R^n$, $\mu(x) = \{y \in {}^*R^n | y \simeq x\}$.

LEMMA 1.

(a) *If* $\} \in {}^*\mathcal{P}$, *then* $\mathfrak{z}$ *is near-standard;*
(b) *If* $\} \in {}^*\mathcal{P}$, *then* ${}^o\mathfrak{z}$, *the standard part of* $\mathfrak{z}$, *is* $\{\langle {}^o x, {}^o y\rangle | x \mathfrak{z} y$, *x and y finite*$\}$;
(c) $(\forall \} \in {}^*\mathcal{P})$ $(\forall$ *finite* $x, y \in {}^*R^n_+)$ $\{[(\forall w \simeq x)(\forall z \simeq y) w \} z] \leftrightarrow {}^o x \, {}^o\} \, {}^o y\}$.

PROOF. (a) follows from the compactness of $\langle \mathcal{P}, \tau_c \rangle$ and Robinson's nonstandard characterization of compact topological spaces (Robinson, 1974, Thm. 4.13).

(b) is a direct consequence of Theorem 3.3 in Narens (1972).

(c) If $(\forall y \in A)(\forall z \in B) y \} z$, then we will write $A \} B$. If $\} \in {}^*\mathcal{P}$, x and y finite and $\mu(x) \} \mu(y)$, then there exists a standard number δ such that $B_\delta(x) \} B_\delta(y)$, where $B_\delta(z)$ is the ball of radius δ centered at z. Hence, by transfer there exists $\}_n$ such that $\lim \mathfrak{z}_n = {}^o\mathfrak{z}$ and $B_\delta({}^o x) \}_n B_\delta({}^o y)$. Therefore, ${}^o x \, {}^o\} \, {}^o y$. If $\} \in {}^*\mathcal{P}$, x and y finite and $(\forall w \simeq x)(\forall z \simeq y)$ such that $w \mathfrak{z} z$, then by transfer there exists x_n, y_n where $x_n \to {}^o x$, $y_n \to {}^o y$, $(\forall n \in N) x_n \mathfrak{z}_n y_n$ and $\lim \mathfrak{z}_n = {}^o\mathfrak{z}$. Hence ${}^o x \, {}^o\mathfrak{z} \, {}^o y$.

B. We also require various concepts from nonstandard measure theory. A nonstandard infinitesimal measure space is a 3-tuple (T, ϕ, ν), where $T = \{1, \ldots, \omega\}$, with $\omega \in {}^*N - N$, ϕ is the algebra of all internal subsets of T, and ν is a finitely additive infinitesimal measure on ϕ—that is, $\nu(t) \simeq 0$, and $\nu(t) \geq 0$, $\forall t \in T$.

Recent work by Loeb (1975) shows that if T is considered as a standard set, then by using the Caratheodory construction, we can extend ν to a real valued σ-additive measure μ on M, the smallest standard σ-algebra containing α. Furthermore, if an internal function f is α-measurable, then the standard part of f, ${}^o f$, is M-measurable and, if f and μ are standardly bounded, then the ν-integral of f is infinitesimally close to the μ-integral of ${}^o f$. More formally, if we define $\mu(A) = {}^o[\nu(A)]$, for all $A \in \alpha$, then the next four results are established in Loeb (1975). Also see Anderson (1981).

THEOREM 1. *The extended real-valued function* μ *has a standard,* σ*-additive extension to the smallest (external)* σ*-algebra* M *in* T *containing* α. *For each* $B \in M$, *the value of this extension is given by* $\mu(B) = \inf_{A\in\phi, B\subseteq A} \mu(A)$ *and there is an* $A \in \phi$ *with* $\mu(B - A)\backslash(A - B) = 0$.

THEOREM 2. *If* $f: T \to {}^*R$ *is* α*-measurable, then* ${}^\circ f: T \to R\nu \cup \{+\infty\}$, *where* ${}^\circ f(t) = {}^\circ[f(t)]$, $t \in T$, *is* M*-measurable. (Loeb observes that Theorem 2 can be extended to the case of an internal mapping* f *from* X *into the extension* $^*Z$ *of a compact metric space* Z *with metric* d.)

THEOREM 3. *Assume that* $\mu(T) < +\infty$, *and let* $f: T \to {}^*[-n, n]$, $n \in N$, *be* α*-measurable. Then for each* $A \in \alpha$, $\int {}^\circ f d\mu \simeq \int f d\nu$.

PROPOSITION 1 (L. C. MOORE, JR.). *Assume* $\mu(T) < +\infty$. *If* $g: T \to R$ *is* M*-measurable, then there is an* $f: T \to {}^*R$ *which is* α*-measurable, such that* ${}^\circ f = g$ *almost everywhere with respect to* μ.

Whereas the theorems of Loeb tell us how to move from a nonstandard measure space to a standard measure space, the proposition of Moore enables us to move the other way—Moore's proposition is a partial converse to Theorem 2 of Loeb.

LEMMA 2. *The measure* μ *on* M *derived by using Loeb's construction is nonatomic if* ν *is an infinitesimal measure.*

PROOF. Without loss of generality, we assume that ν is a uniform counting measure—that is, $\nu(A) = |A|/|T|$ for $A \in \alpha$. Suppose μ atomic. Then there exists $B \in M$ such that $\mu(B) > 0$ and either $\mu(A) = \mu(B)$ or $\mu(A) = 0$, $A \subseteq B$.

By Theorem 1 of Loeb, we know that we can approximate B from within by sets in α. Hence there exists $A \in \alpha$ such that $\nu(A) = \mu(B) > 0$. But A is a *finite collection of points which we can map onto some initial segment of $^*N$, say $\{1, \ldots, n\}$. By picking a subset consisting of $n/2$ points, we obtain $A' \subseteq A$, and $0 < \mu(A') < \mu(A)$.

Bibliography

Bibliographic Note

Among the applications of nonstandard analysis not mentioned in the text, the following are especially deserving of attention.

1. R. M. Anderson shows the metamathematical result that, under appropriate conditions, when two objects almost satisfy a property, they must be near objects that exactly satisfy the property. The paper uses the permanence principle and requires some mathematical logic for full appreciation. "Almost implies near," *Transactions of the American Mathematical Society* (1986).

2. H. J. Kiesler applies his pioneering work on nonstandard stochastic processes to price dynamics in "A price adjustment model with infinitesimal traders," in *Models of Economic Dynamics* (Berlin: Springer-Verlag, 1986). The reader of this book may require some further work before mastering this highly interesting and fruitful topic.

3. Nigel Cutland provides simple, instructive proofs of various known theorems in control theory as well as some new results in his papers. Loeb measure spaces are used, and the correspondence between internal (nonstandard) controls and generalized (standard) controls is noteworthy. "Infinitesimal methods in control theory: Deterministic and Stochastic," *Acta Applicande Mathematicae* (forthcoming, 1986).

4. K. J. Stroyan gives an elegant characterization of myopia over infinite consumption streams in discrete time (ℓ_∞). The paper is an outgrowth of Stroyan's characterization of the Mackey topology. "Myopic utility functions on sequential economies," *Journal of Mathematical Economics* (1983) 11, 3: 267–76.

Anderson, R. M. 1978. "An elementary core equivalence theorem." *Econometrica* 46: 1483–87.

———. 1981. "Core theory with strongly convex preferences." *Econometrica* 49: 1457–68.

———. 1982. "Star-finite representations of measure spaces." *Transactions of the American Mathematical Society* 217: 667–87.

———. 1982. "A market value approach to approximate equilibria." *Econometrica* 50: 127-36.

Anderson, R. M., M. A. Khan, and S. Rashid. 1982. "Approximate equilibria with bounds independent of preference." *Review of Economic Studies* 44: 473-75.

Anderson, R. M., and S. Rashid. 1978. "A nonstandard characterisation of weak convergence." *Proceedings of the American Mathematical Society* 69: 327-32.

Armstrong, T., and M. K. Richter. 1983. "Existence of nonatomic Core-Walras allocations." Mimeographed.

———. 1984. "The Core-Walras equivalence." *Journal of Economic Theory* 33: 116-51.

Arrow, K. J. 1951. "An extension of the basic theorems of classical welfare economics." In J. Neyman, ed., *Proceedings of the Second Berkeley Symposium on Mathematical Statistics and Probability*. Berkeley and Los Angeles: University of California Press, pp. 507-32.

———. 1952. "The determination of many commodity preferences by two-commodity comparisons." *Metroeconomica* 4: 105-15.

Arrow, K. J., and G. Debreu. 1954. "Existence of equilibrium for a competitive economy." *Econometrica* 22: 265-90.

Arrow, K. J., and F. H. Hahn. 1971. *General Competitive Analysis*. San Francisco: Holden-Day.

Arrow, K. J., and M. D. Intrilligator, eds. 1982. *Handbook of Mathematical Economics*. Amsterdam: North Holland.

Aumann, R. J. 1964. "Markets with a continuum of traders." *Econometrica* 32: 39-50.

———. 1966. "Existence of competitive equilibria in markets with a continuum of traders." *Econometrica* 34: 1-17.

———. 1969. "Measurable utility and the measurable choice theorem." *La Decision*, Collogue Internationaux du C.N.R.S., Paris, pp. 15-26.

———. 1973. "Disadvantageous monopolies." *Journal of Economic Theory* 6: 1-11.

———. 1975. "Values of markets with a continuum of traders." *Econometrica* 43: 611-46.

Aumann, R. J., and L. S. Shapley. 1974. *Values of Non-Atomic Games*. Princeton: Princeton University Press.

Bator, F. M. 1961. "Convexity, efficiency and markets." *Journal of Political Economy* 69: 480-83; and "Rejoinder." Ibid., 489.

Berge, C. 1966. *Espaces Topologigues*. 2d ed. Paris: Dunod.

Bewley, C. 1972. "Existence of equilibria in economies with infinitely many commodities." *Journal of Economic Theory* 4: 514-40.

———. 1974. "Edgeworth's conjecture." *Econometrica* 41: 415-52.

Billingsley, P. 1968. *Convergence of Probability Measures.* New York: Wiley.

Bledsoe, A. T. 1868. *Philosophy of Mathematics*. Philadelphia: Lippincott.

Bohm, V. 1973. "On cores and equilibria of productive economies with a measure space of consumers: An example." *Journal of Economic Theory* 6: 409-12.

Broome, J. 1972. "Existence of equilibrium in economies with indivisible commodities." *Journal of Economic Theory* 5: 224-50.

Brown, D. J. 1973. "The core of a purely competitive economy." Mimeographed.

———. 1976. "Existence of competitive equilibrium in a nonstandard exchange economy." *Econometrica* 44: 537–47.

———. 1977. "Nonstandard economies: A survey." Mimeographed.

Brown, D. J., and M. A. Khan. 1980. "An extension of the Brown-Robinson equivalence theorem." *Applied Mathematics and Computation* 6: 167–75.

Brown, D. J., and L. Lewis. 1981. "Myopic economic agents." *Econometrica* 49: 359–68.

Brown, D. J., and P. A. Loeb. 1976. "The values of nonstandard exchange economies." *Israel Journal of Mathematics* 25: 71–86.

Brown, D. J., and A. Robinson. 1972. "A limit theorem on the cores of large standard exchange economies." *Proceedings of the National Academy of Sciences of the U.S.A.* 69: 1258–60, Correction, 69: 3068.

———. 1974. "The cores of large standard exchange economies." *Journal of Economic Theory* 9: 245–54.

———. 1975. "Nonstandard exchange economies." *Econometrica* 43: 41–55.

Cassels, J. W. S. 1975. "Measures of the non-convexity of sets and the Shapley-Folkman-Starr theorem." *Mathematical Proceedings, Cambridge Philosophical Society* 78: 433–36.

Chipman, J. S., L. Hurwicz, M. K. Richter, and H. F. Sonnenschein, eds. 1971. *Preferences, Utility, and Demand.* New York: Harcourt Brace Jovanovich.

Cornwall, R. 1969. "The use of prices to characterize the core of an economy." *Journal of Economic Theory* 1: 353–73.

Cramer, H. 1946. *Mathematical Methods of Statistics.* Princeton: Princeton University Press.

Davis, M. 1977. *Applied Nonstandard Analysis.* New York: Wiley.

Debreu, G. 1952. "A social equilibrium existence theorem." *Proceedings of the National Academy of Sciences of U.S.A.* 38: 886–93.

———. 1954. "Valuation equilibrium and Pareto optimum." *Proceedings of the National Academy of Sciences of U.S.A.* 40: 588–92.

———. 1956. "Market equilibrium." *Proceedings of the National Academy of Sciences of U.S.A.* 42: 876–78.

———. 1959. *Theory of Value.* New York: Wiley.

———. 1962. "New concepts and techniques for equilibrium analysis." *International Economic Review* 3: 257–73.

———. 1963. "On a theorem of Scarf." *Review of Economic Studies* 30: 177–80.

———. 1967. "Preference functions on a measure space of economic agents." *Econometrica* 35: 111–22.

Debreu, G., and H. Scarf. 1963. "A limit theorem on the core of an economy." *International Economic Review* 4: 235–46.

Dierker, E. 1971. "Equilibrium analysis of exchange economies with indivisible commodities." *Econometrica* 39: 997–1008.

Dreze, J. H., S. Gepts, and J. Gabszewicz. 1969. "On cores and competitive equilibria." In *La Decision*, Collogue Internationaux du C.N.R.S., Paris, pp. 91–114.

Edgeworth, F. Y. 1881. *Mathematical Psychics.* London: P. Kegan.

Edwards, C. H. 1979. *The Historical Development of the Calculus.* New York: Springer Verlag.

Emmons, D. 1984. "Existence of Lindahl equilibria in measure-theoretic economies without ordered preferences." *Journal of Economic Theory* 34: 342-59.

Farrell, M. J. 1959. "The convexity assumption in the theory of competitive markets." *Journal of Political Economy* 67: 377-91.

Gabszewicz, J. 1977. "Asymmetric duopoly and the core." *Journal of Economic Theory* 14: 172-79.

Gabszewicz, J., and J. H. Dreze. 1971. "Syndicate of traders in an exchange economy." In H. W. Kuhn and G. P. Szego, eds., *Differential Games and Related Topics*. Amsterdam: North Holland, pp. 399-414.

Gabszewicz, J., and J. F. Mertens. 1971. "An equivalence theorem for the core of an economy whose atoms are not 'too' big." *Econometrica* 39: 713-21.

Gabszewicz, J., and J. P. Vial. 1972. "Oligopoly 'a la Cournot' in a general equilibrium analysis." *Journal of Economic Theory* 4: 381-400.

Gale, D. 1955. "The law of supply and demand." *Mathematica Scandinavica* 3: 155-69.

Genakopoulos, J. 1978. "The bargaining set and nonstandard analysis." Harvard University. Mimeographed.

Georgescu-Roegen, N. 1979. "Methods in economic science." *Journal of Economic Issues* 15: 317-28; and "Reply." *Ibid.* 17(1981): 187-91.

Green, J. R. 1972. "On the inequitable nature of core allocations." *Journal of Economic Theory* 4: 132-43.

Greenberg, J., and B. Shitovitz. 1977. "Disadvantageous monopolies." *Journal of Economic Theory* 16: 394-402.

Grodal, B. 1972. "A second remark on the core of an atomless economy." *Econometrica* 40: 581-83.

———. 1974. "A note on the space of preference relations." *Journal of Mathematical Economics* 1: 279-94.

Hart, S., and E. Kohlberg. 1974. "Equally distributed correspondences." *Journal of Mathematical Economics* 1: 167-74.

Hart, S., W. Hildenbrand, and E. Kohlberg. 1974. "On equilibrium allocations as distributions in the commodity space." *Journal of Mathematical Economics* 1: 159-66.

Henle, J. M., and E. M. Kleinberg. 1979. *Infinitesimal Calculus.* Cambridge, Mass.: MIT Press.

Hildenbrand, W. 1968. "The core of an economy with a measure space of economic agents." *Review of Economic Studies* 35: 443-52.

———. 1969. "Pareto optimality for a measure space of economic agents." *International Economic Review* 10: 363-72.

———. 1970a. "On economies with many agents." *Journal of Economic Theory* 2: 161-88.

———. 1970b. "Existence of equilibria for economies with production and a measure space of consumers." *Econometrica* 38: 608-23.

———. 1971. "Random preferences and equilibrium analysis." *Journal of Economic Theory* 4: 414-29.

———. 1972. "Measure spaces of economic agents." In L. LeCam, J. Neyman, and E. L. Scott, eds., *Proceedings of the Sixth Berkeley Symposium on Mathematical Statistics and Probability.* Berkeley and Los Angeles: University of California Press, pp. 41-56.

———. 1974. *Core and Equilibria of a Large Economy.* Princeton: Princeton University Press.

———. 1982. "The core of an economy." In K. J. Arrow and M. D. Intrilligator, eds., *Handbook of Mathematical Economics.* Amsterdam: North Holland.

Hildenbrand, W., and A. P. Kirman. 1973. "Size removes inequality." *Review of Economic Studies* 30: 305–14.

Hildenbrand, W., D. Schmeidler, and S. Zamir. 1973. "Existence of approximate equilibria and cores." *Econometrica* 41: 1159–66.

Hrbacek, K. 1979. "Nonstandard set theory." *American Mathematical Monthly* 79: 659–77.

Hurd, A. E., and P. A. Loeb. 1985. *An Introduction to Nonstandard Real Analysis.* New York: Academic Press.

Kannai, Y. 1970. "Continuity properties of the core of a market." *Econometrica* 38: 791–815.

———. 1972. "Continuity properties of the core of a market: A correction." *Econometrica* 40: 955–58.

Karlin, S. 1959. *Mathematical Method and Theory in Game, Programming and Economics.* Vol. 2. Reading, Mass.: Addison-Wesley.

Khan, M. A. 1973. "Large Exchange Economies." Ph.D. dissertation, Yale University.

———. 1974a. "Some equivalence theorems." *Review of Economic Studies* 61: 549–65.

———. 1974b. "Approximately convex average sum of unbounded sets." *Proceedings of the American Mathematical Society* 43: 181–85.

———. 1975. "Some approximate equilibria." *Journal of Mathematical Economics* 2: 63–86.

———. 1976. "Oligopoly in markets with a continuum of traders: An asymptotic interpretation." *Journal of Economic Theory* 12: 273–97.

———. 1977a. "Some remarks on sets with unbounded nonconvexities." *Metroeconomica* 29: 149–58.

———. 1977b. "On the core of an economy whose atoms are not 'too big.'" Unpublished.

———. 1981. "Approximate convexity of average sums of sets in normed linear spaces." *Applied Mathematics and Computation* 9: 27–34.

Khan, M. A., and H. Polemarchakis. 1978. "Unequal treatment in the core." *Econometrica* 46: 1475–81.

Khan, M. A., and S. Rashid. 1975. "Pareto optimality and nonconvexity in large markets." *International Economic Review* 16: 222–45.

———. 1977. "Limit theorems in cores with costs of coalition formation." Johns Hopkins University Working Paper 28. Rev. ed.

———. 1978. "A limit theorem for an approximate core." *Economics Letters* 1: 297–302.

———. 1982. "Approximate equilibria in markets with indivisible commodities." *Journal of Economic Theory* 28: 82–101.

Khan, M. A., and A. Yamazaki. 1981. "On the cores of economies with indivisible commodities and a continuum of traders." *Journal of Economic Theory* 24: 218–25.

Kiesler, M. J. 1984. *An Infinitesimal Approach to Stochastic Analysis.* Memoirs of the American Mathematical Society, no. 297, Providence, R.I.

Kleen, C. 1980. "Pure competition in the case of countably many traders." *Methods of Operations Research* 36: 195-202.

Koopmans, T. C. 1951. "Analysis of production as an efficient combination of activities." In T. C. Koopmans, ed., *Activity Analysis of Production and Allocation*. New York: Wiley, pp. 33-97.

———. 1961. "Convexity assumptions, allocative efficiency, and competitive equilibrium." *Journal of Political Economy* 69: 478-79.

Lewis, L. 1977. "Essays on Purely Competitive Intertemporal Exchange." Ph.D. dissertation, Yale University.

Loeb, P. A. 1972. "A nonstandard representation of measurable spaces, L_∞ and $*L_\infty$." In W. A. J. Luxemburg and A. Robinson, eds., *Contributions to Nonstandard Analysis*. Amsterdam: North-Holland, pp. 65-80.

———. 1973. "A combinatorial analogue of Lyapunov's theorem for infinitesimally generated atomic vector measures." *Proceedings of the American Mathematical Society* 39: 585-86.

———. 1975. "Conversion from nonstandard to standard measure spaces and applications in potential theory." *Transactions of the American Mathematical Society* 211: 113-22.

———. 1979a. "Weak limits of measures and the standard part map." *Proceedings of the American Mathematical Society* 77: 128-35.

———. 1979b. "An introduction to nonstandard analysis and hyperfinite probability theory." *Probabilistic Analysis and Related Topics.* Vol. 2. New York: Academic Press.

Luxemburg, W. A. J. 1973. "What is nonstandard analysis." *American Mathematical Monthly* 18: 38-67.

Lyapunov, A. 1940. "Sur les fonctions-vecteurs complement additives." *Bulletin of the Academy of Sciences URSS* (Mathematics) 4: 465-78.

Marchi, E. 1967. "On the minimax theorem of the theory of games." *Annali de Mathematica pura ed Applicata* 77: 207-82.

Marchi, E., and P. Tarazaga. 1977. "The minimax theorem for continuous games using an elimination procedure." *International Journal of Game Theory* 6: 115-21.

Mas-Colell, A. 1974. "An equilibrium existence theorem without complete or transitive preferences." *Journal of Mathematical Economics* 1: 237-46.

———. 1977. "Indivisible commodities and general equilibrium theory." *Journal of Economic Theory* 16: 443-56.

McKenzie, L. 1954. "On equilibrium in Graham's model of world trade and other competitive systems." *Econometrica* 22: 147-61.

———. 1959. "On the existence of general equilibrium for a competitive market." *Econometrica* 27: 54-71.

Narens, L. 1972. "Topologies of closed subsets." *Transactions of the American Mathematical Society* 174: 55-76.

Nikaido, H. 1968. *Convex Structures and Economic Theory.* New York: Academic Press.

Nomura, M. 1984. "Essays on economies with infinitely many commodities." Ph.D. dissertation, Johns Hopkins University.

Rashid, S. 1976. "Economies with infinitely many traders." Ph.D. dissertation, Yale University.
———. 1978. "Existence of equilibrium in infinite economies with production." *Econometrica* 46: 1155–64.
———. 1979. "The relationship between measure-theoretic and nonstandard exchange economies." *Journal of Mathematical Economics* 6: 195–202.
———. 1983. "Equilibrium points of non-atomic games: Asymptotic results." *Economics Letters* 12: 7–10.
Richter, H. 1963. "Verallgemlinerung eines in der Statistik benatigten Satzes der Masstheorie." *Mathematische Annalen* 150: 85–90, Beweiserganzung, 440–41.
Richter, M. K. 1971. "Coalition core and competition." *Journal of Economic Theory* 3: 323–34.
Roberts, D. J., and A. Postlewaite. 1976. "The incentives for price-taking behavior in large exchange economies." *Econometrica* 44: 115–27.
Robinson, A. 1974. *Nonstandard Analysis*. 2d ed. New York: American Elsevier.
Rockafellar, R. T. 1970. *Convex Analysis*. Princeton: Princeton University Press.
Rothenberg, J. 1960. "Non-convexity, aggregation, and Pareto optimality." *Journal of Political Economy* 68: 435–68; and "Comments on Non-Convexity." *Ibid.* 69(1961): 490–92.
Royden, H. L. 1963. *Real Analysis*. London: Macmillan.
Scarf, H. 1962. "An analysis of markets with a large number of participants." In M. Maschler, ed., *Recent Advances in Game Theory*. Princeton: Privately printed.
———. 1967. "The core of an *n*-person game." *Econometrica* 35: 50–69.
Schmeidler, D. 1969. "Competitive equilibria in markets with a continuum of traders and incomplete preferences." *Econometrica* 37: 578–85.
———. 1972. "A remark on the core of an atomless economy." *Econometrica* 40: 579–80.
Shaked, A. 1976. "Absolute approximations to equilibrium in markets with non-convex preferences." *Journal of Mathematical Economics* 3: 185–96.
Shapley, L. S. 1975. "An example of a slow converging core." *International Economic Review* 16: 345–51.
Shapley, L. S., and M. Shubik. 1966. "Quasi-cores in a monetary economy with non-convex preferences." *Econometrica* 34: 805–27.
Shitovitz, B. 1974a. "Oligopoly in markets with a continuum of traders." *Econometrica* 41: 467–501.
———. 1974b. "On some problems arising in markets with some large traders and a continuum of small traders." *Journal of Economic Theory* 8: 458–70.
———. 1982. "Some notes on the core of a production economy with some large traders and a continuum of small traders." *Journal of Mathematical Economics* 9: 99–105.
Shubik, M. 1959. "Edgeworth market games." In R. D. Luce and A. W. Tucker, eds., *Contributions to the Theory of Games*. Vol. 4, *Annals of Mathematical Studies*, no. 40. Princeton: Princeton University Press, pp. 267–78.
Skala, H. 1974. "Nonstandard utilities and the foundation of game theory." *International Journal of Game Theory* 3: 67–81.

Sondermann, D. 1975. "Economics of scale and equilibria in coalition production economies." *Journal of Economic Theory* 8: 259-91.

Starr, R. M. 1969. "Quasi-equilibria in markets with non-convex preferences." *Econometrica* 37: 25-38.

———. 1981. "Approximation of points of the convex hull of a sum of sets by points of the sum: An elementary approach." *Journal of Economic Theory* 25: 314-17.

Steinitz, E. 1913. "Bedingle konvergente Reihen und Convexe Systems." *Journal a für Mathematike* 143: 128-75.

Stigler, G. J. 1957. "Perfect competition, historically contemplated." *Journal of Political Economy* 65: 1-17.

Stroyan, K., and W. J. Luxemburg. 1976. *Introduction to the Theory of Infinitesimals.* New York: Academic Press.

Temple, G. 1981. *100 Years of Mathematics.* London: Duckworth, pp. 19-25.

Trockel, W. 1976. "A limit theorem on the core." *Journal of Mathematical Economics* 3: 247-64.

Vind, K. 1964. "Edgeworth-allocations in an exchange economy with many traders." *International Economic Review* 5: 165-77.

———. 1965. "A theorem on the core of an economy." *Review of Economic Studies* 5: 165-77.

———. 1973. "A third remark on the core of an atomless economy." *Econometrica* 40: 585-86.

Waismann, F. 1951. *Introduction to Mathematical Thinking.* New York: F. Unger, pp. 220-23.

Walras, L. 1874. *Elements d'economie politique pure.* Lausanne: L. Corbaz.

Weddepohl, C. 1977. "Equilibrium in a market with incomplete preferences where the number of consumers may be finite." In G. Schwodiauer, ed., *Equilibrium and Disequilibrium in Economic Theory.* Dordrecht: Reidel, pp. 15-26.

Wesley, E. 1971. "An application of nonstandard analysis to game theory." *Journal of Symbolic Logic* 36: 385-94.

Yamazaki, A. 1978. "An equilibrium existence theorem without convexity assumptions." *Econometrica* 46: 541-55.

———. 1981. "Diversified consumption characteristic and conditionally dispersed endowment distribution: Regularizing effect theorems." *Econometrica* 49: 639-55.

Yannelis, N. C. 1980. "Approximate equilibrium in large economies." Johns Hopkins Working Paper 68.

Zieba, E. 1957. "An elementary proof of Von-Neumann's minimax theorem." *Colloquium Mathematica* 6: 224-26.

Subject Index

Author Index

About the Author

Salim Rashid is professor of economics at the University of Illinois, Urbana-Champaign. He is the author of numerous articles published in the professional literature of economics.

Economies with Many Agents

Designed by Martha Farlow

Composed by Action Comp Co., Inc., in English Times

Printed by BookCrafters on 50-lb. S. D. Warren's Sebago Eggshell Cream offset paper and bound in Joanna Arrestox cloth